Almost Astronauts

Almost Astronauts
13 Women Who Dared to Dream

TANYA LEE STONE

CANDLEWICK PRESS

**For the extraordinary women in my family,
beginning with Bessie, Sarah, Leah, and Dorothy —
all the way to Laurie, Sarah, Leah, and Liza**

A Note about "Mercury 13"
The "Mercury 13" is actually a misnomer, as these thirteen women were never part of the Mercury space program. But because they went through many of the same tests that the Mercury astronauts did, the "Mercury 13" has become the nickname most often associated with the women in this story.

Text copyright © 2009 by Tanya Lee Stone
Photography credits appear on page 131.

First paperback edition 2009

The Library of Congress has cataloged the hardcover edition as follows:
Stone, Tanya Lee.
Almost astronauts : 13 women who dared to dream / by Tanya Lee Stone. — 1st ed.
p. cm.
Includes biographical references.
ISBN 978-0-7636-3611-1
1. Women astronauts — United States — Biography — Juvenile literature.
2. Women astronauts — United States — History — 20th century — Juvenile literature.
3. Sex discrimination against women — United States — History — 20th Century —
Juvenile literature. 4. Project Mercury (U.S.) — History — Juvenile literature. I. Title.
TL789.85.A1S79 2008
629.450092'273 — dc22   2008017487

ISBN 978-0-7636-4502-1 (paperback)

2 4 6 8 10 9 7 5 3 1

Printed in the United States of America

This book was typeset in Utopia.

Candlewick Press
99 Dover Street
Somerville, Massachusetts 02144

visit us at www.candlewick.com

Women must try to do things as men have tried. When they fail, their failure must be but a challenge to others.

— *Amelia Earhart, in a letter she wrote shortly before disappearing on her final flight*

The world was divided into those who had it and those who did not. This quality, this *it,* was never named. . . . The idea was to prove . . . that you were one of the elected and anointed ones who had *the right stuff.*

— *Tom Wolfe, from his novel* The Right Stuff, *about the Mercury 7 astronauts*

Contents

Foreword by Margaret A. Weitekamp   ix

Chapter 1: T Minus Thirty-Eight Years   1

Chapter 2: I Jumped at the Offer   7

Chapter 3: NOT a Meaningful Test   23

Chapter 4: Mommy's Going to the Moon!   35

Chapter 5: Too Good to Be True   45

Chapter 6: Regret to Advise . . .   53

Chapter 7: Let's Stop This Now!   59

Chapter 8: Jerrie Cobb Isn't Running This Program. I Am!   67

Chapter 9: The Men Go Off and Fight the Wars and Fly the Airplanes   77

Chapter 10: NASA Never Had any Intention of Putting Those Women in Space   87

Chapter 11: We Want to See a Woman Driving the Bus, Not Sitting in the Back   95

Chapter 12: I Am Living Proof That Dreams Do Come True   105

Author's Note   119

Appendix   122

Further Reading   123

Webliography   123

Sources   123

Source Notes   127

Photography Credits   131

Index   132

Acknowledgments   134

Foreword

Whenever I give a public talk about the Lovelace Woman in Space program and the women pilots who took astronaut fitness tests in the early 1960s, inevitably someone in the crowd asks me if there is a book about these women that is suitable for young people.

Often the questioner has a daughter, or a granddaughter, or a niece who excels at math and science or who is excited about aviation and space. She is a girl whom they would like to encourage with new role models. The women in this book are those examples: pilots who dreamed about the possibilities of spaceflight many years before that opportunity was open to them.

Sometimes the person who is asking wants to give the book to a boy. They want to show him that accomplished women and men stand on the shoulders of visionaries who pushed the boundaries of what was possible. This is that history.

With clear writing, engaging characters, and compelling events, Tanya Lee Stone brings this history to life. And she does so while offering nuanced historical arguments in simple language. Young people will appreciate that she does not talk down to them.

I'm looking forward to the next time that I'm asked to recommend an accessible book on this topic—because I finally have a satisfactory answer. Yes! This is that book.

Margaret A. Weitekamp
Curator, National Air and Space Museum
Smithsonian Institution

Chapter 1

T Minus Thirty-Eight Years

July 1999

One woman stands alone, off to the side of the crowd.

She paces back and forth—agitated, excited, impatient.

From the back, it is hard to tell her age; her faded brown leather jacket and blond ponytail reveal nothing. But if she were to turn to glance at the group of women on the observation bleachers behind her, you would see the lines of time etched on her face. You would see a smile tinged with sadness.

Although the women behind her huddle close like sisters, sharing a chuckle, a tease here and there, a knowing look, it is not at her expense. They understand her need for solitude. This is an emotional time for all of them, but perhaps especially for her, Jerrie Cobb.

It was Jerrie who led them in a quest to live their dreams, Jerrie who first believed they had a shot at all this, Jerrie who still, to this day, is fighting for her dream.

Nearly forty years earlier, it was Jerrie who thought she would be exactly where Eileen Collins is right now: inside a NASA craft, about to fly into space.

The crew of the STS-93 mission has been briefed. They've suited up and waved to the cameras on their walk out to the launchpad. They're on board the space shuttle, checking and rechecking their equipment, making sure all systems are go. The astronauts are ready.

The space shuttle *Columbia* awaits the launch of mission STS-93.

Lieutenant Colonel Eileen Collins is in charge. This is the first time a woman has ever been the commander of a space shuttle—has ever sat in the "driver's seat."

The thousands upon thousands of spectators who have come to get a glimpse of the action line their cars along the sides of the highway all around Cape Canaveral and crowd onto the beaches.

But Jerrie Cobb and the others are situated directly across the Banana River from the launchpad. This is as close as it gets. Only family and friends of the astronauts and VIP guests are invited to watch shuttle launches from this coveted spot. When Collins made her first launch, in 1995, she asked NASA to roll out the red carpet for the "Mercury 13" women, and the agency agreed. They were given behind-the-scenes tours and introduced to space experts who had never heard their story. One of the women who attended, Gene Nora Stumbough Jessen, is missing today's launch to be at the opening of the new Ninety-Nines Museum of Women Pilots. But many other women pilots are here, including Women Airforce Service Pilots (WASP, the first female pilots to fly military aircraft during World War II), Whirly-Girls (the first organization of female helicopter pilots), and pioneering air-race champions.

None, though, have closer personal ties to this historic event than Jerrie Cobb and her group. Nearly forty years ago, it was almost them. They were almost astronauts.

And for a little while, that dream placed them on the same path together. It was a path that helped shape their personal stories as well as the bigger, ongoing, living and breathing tale that is our American history.

A shuttle launch is a complicated thing. Conditions must be perfect. This time, foul weather triggers a delay, so the crowds head off the Cape, scrambling onto Greyhound buses and winding the long way back to Cocoa Beach. Jerrie Cobb and her group set off together, with Jerrie remaining quiet, taking part only occasionally in the chatter.

Their original group was thirteen. Of the eleven surviving members, eight are gathered today. Four of them—Jerri Sloan Truhill, Bernice "B" Steadman, Rhea Hurrle Woltman, and Sarah Gorelick Ratley—scheduled their flights to Orlando so that they would arrive at about the same time. That way, they could rent a car and drive to the Cape as a posse, checking into one big motel room. They like to bunk together, stay up late talking and catching up on one another's lives since they rarely get the chance. Three others—Jane Hart, Wally Funk, and Irene Leverton—are here as well.

They have all settled into a coffee shop in Cocoa Beach to wait out the delay. Jerri Truhill entertains them with boisterous stories of her days as a young pilot, recalling

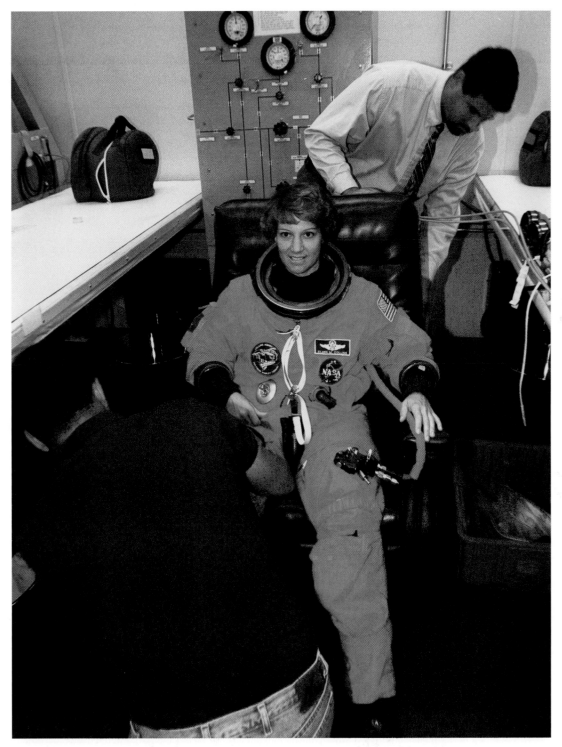

Eileen Collins, the first woman to command a space shuttle, gets help suiting up for launch.

The STS-93 crew waves to the crowd on their way to the shuttle. The five crew members are (starting from rear, left to right) Mission Specialists Michel Tognini and Catherine G. Coleman, Pilot Jeffrey S. Ashby, Mission Specialist Steven A. Hawley, and Commander Eileen M. Collins.

the shock on a man's face one day when she took off her helmet, revealing the fact that she was a woman.

They know exactly what she's describing; it's happened to all of them. They laugh along with Jerri, caught up in her infectious guffaws. You don't have to wonder what Jerri thinks about things. She's a woman who doesn't hold back, speaking her mind without hesitation. Despite being in her seventies, she is still every inch the rebel, not afraid to take chances. None of them are.

It was 1961 when they took their shot at being astronauts. Back then, women weren't allowed to rent a car or take out a loan from the bank without a man's signature; they could not play on a professional sports team at all. They couldn't report the news on television or run in a city marathon or serve as police officers. They weren't allowed to fly jets, either. And these are just some of the bigger examples.

None of that kept these women from trying to be astronauts. They were too determined. Every single one of them shared a common dream from the time they were little girls: they were all born to fly.

The Countdown Continues

Back in the stands for another launch attempt, they wait for the countdown, and hope. They hope all goes off without a hitch. They hope that this time, the wait will have been worth it.

STS-93 is ready.

Eileen Collins is ready.

Wally Funk yells, "Go, Eileen! Go for all of us!"

The crowd tenses.

The clock counts down.

Nine . . . eight . . . seven . . .

The illuminated numbers on the enormous digital clock stop.

There is a technical problem. Another delay.

Someone in the crowd complains loudly, "T minus six seconds!"

Jerri Sloan Truhill sasses back, "Try T minus thirty-eight years."

Chapter 2

I Jumped at the Offer

1960

We have turned back the clock.

John F. Kennedy has just been elected president.

Three years earlier, the Soviet Union (now Russia) launched a satellite called Sputnik. It was the first time anyone, anywhere, had sent *anything* into orbit around Earth. People all over the world were talking about it. The United States was determined to get into the game.

And it did. In 1958, the year after Sputnik went up, the National Aeronautics and Space Administration (NASA) was created. President Kennedy put beating the Russians in the race to explore space right at the top of his to-do list.

NASA put together a winning team for their Mercury program—a program designed to orbit a man around Earth. Seven male jet test pilots, the best of the best, went through extensive testing and training to be selected as the first group of American astronauts.

They were dubbed the Mercury 7 and hailed as heroes. Their faces beamed out from the September 14, 1959, cover of *Life* magazine. The article's headline: THE ASTRONAUTS—READY TO MAKE HISTORY. Confident, strong, clean-cut men ready to take on the world. And beyond.

This is what bravery looked like.

The Mercury 7 astronauts. Left to right at front: Walter M. "Wally" Schirra, Donald K. "Deke" Slayton, John H. Glenn Jr., and Scott Carpenter. Left to right at rear: Alan B. Shepard Jr., Virgil I. "Gus" Grissom, and L. Gordon Cooper Jr.

On May 25, 1961, President John F. Kennedy gave a historic speech declaring, "I believe that this nation should commit itself to achieving the goal, before this decade is out, of landing a man on the moon and returning him safely to the earth." In the background are (left) Vice President Lyndon B. Johnson and (right) Speaker of the House Sam T. Rayburn.

When the author Tom Wolfe wrote about these men, he called his book *The Right Stuff*. It was a phrase he coined to describe a quality that jet test pilots and those first astronauts seemed to embody. Men who continually risked their lives to test the boundaries of what new aircraft and spacecraft could do, who were ready to die in the name of their mission, their country. Wolfe wrote, "But it was not bravery in the simple sense of being willing to risk your life. The idea seemed to be that any fool could do that. . . . No, the idea here . . . seemed to be that a man should have the ability to go up in a hurtling piece of machinery and put his hide on the line and then have the moxie, the reflexes, the experience, the coolness, to pull it back in the last yawning moment—and then to go up again *the next day,* and the next day, and every next day. . . . *Manliness, manhood, manly courage* . . . there was something ancient, primordial, irresistible about the challenge of this stuff."

On September 21, another smiling group shot graced the cover of *Life:* the seven wives of the seven astronauts. Their tagline: "Astronauts' Wives: Their Inner Thoughts, Worries." The women talked about how they shared their hopes and fears with one another. Interior photos showed them doing many wifely, motherly chores: bathing the kids, doing dishes, riding bikes with their children, playing cards, and waiting for their husbands to return. They even posed by a full-scale red steel model of the space capsule.

This is what loyalty looked like.

It was a nice, neat package that the media presented. Women in their proper place, supporting their menfolk, keeping the home fires burning.

Of course, these images did not represent all women—especially after World War II. In the 1930s, as many Americans struggled to make a living, most white Americans believed that women shouldn't work unless they had to, shouldn't take jobs away from the men. Certainly, that did not apply to all—African-American women, for example, especially in the South, often worked for white families, and the poorest families, black or white, expected daughters to help out in any way they could. Yet

During World War II, the government created posters such as this one to encourage women to do their part and join the Women's Army Corps (WAC).

"I'm proud of my **two** soldiers"

JOIN THE WAC NOW!

THOUSANDS OF ARMY JOBS NEED FILLING!

Women's Army Corps
United States Army

still, the ideal—the image in the movies and the women's magazines and in common conversation—was of a wife at home who did not work. But the war required an attitude change. Men shipped off and jobs were left open, right when companies desperately needed to increase their productivity. Someone had to keep the factories rolling so that all of the military equipment could be built and sent overseas.

So all different kinds of women, even those who were well off or married, went to work in steel mills, factories, and shipyards. They built boats, planes, and munitions. They joined the Red Cross, the Women's Army Corps (WAC), and the WASP.

Women were called to duty. They jumped in where they were needed. They did their country proud.

Then the men came back from overseas.

And women were called to duty again. But this time, it was to restore the ideal of the traditional family. Even the WASP had their wings clipped; their organization folded. They had proven that women could fly, but the question then became, *Should* they fly? The answer was no. After the war, the men wanted their planes and their jobs back. And they got them.

The Women Airforce Service Pilots (WASP) were considered civil service employees—not military personnel—even though they risked their lives for their country during World War II in noncombat missions, ferrying planes from the factories to the men at military bases overseas.

Most men who had fought in the war wanted to leave that grim scene behind and return to a nice home, a sweet wife, a growing family. As the economy improved, there were more jobs available, and many men were able to support their families on their salaries alone. Many women agreed that their place was the home. But others had tasted independence, had felt the satisfaction of earning their own money, supporting their families, excelling at jobs outside of the home. They didn't want to give all that up and did not like this change in the national mood. They still had hopes and dreams beyond serving up hot casseroles for their men returning home from work. Nevertheless, from the late 1940s through much of the 1950s, these women were viewed as misfits unable to adapt to their "natural" roles.

In 1959, when the Mercury 7 men were put forth as the ideal picture of bravery and heroism, most Americans were ready to agree. But there were women who wanted to see themselves in that same picture—as astronauts on the cover of a magazine.

Enter Randy Lovelace.

Randolph Lovelace was the chairman of NASA's Life Sciences Committee.

Randolph Lovelace was the visionary man behind the Woman in Space program.

He was the doctor who put the Mercury 7 men through all of their testing.

He was a scientist who believed that women are as capable as men, and he wanted to prove it.

Lovelace was a realist, keenly aware that women were often pigeonholed—thought of as interested only in getting married, raising children, and generally being nurturing, pleasant people who wouldn't ruffle too many feathers.

In this social climate, a woman wanting to become an astronaut was going to take a lot of heat. She might even be treated as a joke.

Lovelace knew that if women were ever going to be let into the space program, he was going to have to prove, beyond a shadow of a doubt, not just that they were up to the job but that they were *more than* up to the job. And he believed they were.

He also believed that women could save the space program a lot of money. They are generally smaller and lighter than men, so they need less oxygen and would take up less room in a spacecraft. Female astronauts would be cost-effective, saving NASA nearly $1,000 per pound! But he knew he was going to have a tough time selling NASA on the idea.

Lovelace wasn't the only person to have this same thought. In fact, his was one of three plans being cooked up in 1959 to test women's suitability for spaceflight. This may seem odd, considering the overall status of women at this time, but at least one of the plans—put forward by *Look* magazine—was as much about image as science. The magazine may have been competing with its rival, *Life,* and looking for a fresh story to capture the mood of the nation as it headed toward the new decade, the 1960s. The other two plans had more scientific goals in mind.

Look thought that showing a woman going through some of the astronaut testing would make an interesting magazine story. And NASA cooperated. They allowed a top-notch pilot named Betty Skelton to operate an orbital-flight simulator—a mock spacecraft cockpit. She was then spun around in a centrifuge, a machine that spins a pilot around and around at high speed, preparing him or her for strong acceleration forces in space. She took the tilt-table test, in which she laid on a table that shifted quickly back and forth between flat and upright at a 65-degree angle. She had her body

In addition to setting records as an aerobatic champion, pilot Betty Skelton also broke land speed records in a race car. Her airplane, *Little Stinker*, is on display at the Smithsonian Air and Space Museum.

fluids and functions measured and examined repeatedly. These tests were some of the same tests that men like John Glenn and Scott Carpenter had taken—Mercury 7 men.

When the story ran, Betty Skelton was *Look*'s cover girl, looking fabulous in a sleek silver space suit. The headline read SHOULD A GIRL BE FIRST IN SPACE? Inside, the bulk of the piece was made up of photos of Betty and the Mercury 7 boys joking around—apparently they called her No. 7 1/2—while she took her tests and sported a way-too-large man's flight suit.

None of Skelton's results were included in the article, but, to the writer's credit, he did indicate how well she had done: "She is just a petite example of the anatomical fact that women have more brains and stamina per pound than men." But Skelton was mainly portrayed as soaking up the atmosphere of the male pilots, taking in what they had to teach her, as if she were part of some sort of extravagant career-day presentation. The article also discussed the desired physical and social profile of a female astronaut candidate, saying that she should be "a flat-chested lightweight under thirty-five years of age and married." And it suggested that the best woman for the job might be the "scientist-wife of a pilot," ready to relegate the flying to the men and act as caretaker for the other—presumably male—crew members.

Basically, *Look* was saying that a woman astronaut—if ever a woman might actually be considered—would be a Mommy type who, being married, also wouldn't pose too much of a distraction to the men and whose masculine body type would allow NASA to avoid having to waste precious time designing new space suits just for her.

Would anyone ever suggest that a male astronaut ought to be a married man with little sex appeal? No. Not in a million years. It would be insulting to view a man in this way. This imagined ideal profile of a female astronaut candidate shows the two main ways women were often viewed at the time: they were either curvaceous creatures every man was sure to pursue or safe plain Janes any man could ignore. To some women, the realization that this was still true after women had so clearly proved their worth, strength, and bravery was simply depressing. Skelton later revealed that although the Mercury 7 were welcoming, one top official told her, "Women in space? If I had my way, I would send them all out there!"

In the end, *Look* got their high-interest story and NASA was able to glamorize their space program for the general public. The whole thing was an exercise in public relations. Skelton was never actually considered a potential astronaut candidate by anyone. And she knew it.

So why did she do it? Skelton said, "I felt it was an opportunity to try to convince them that a woman could do this type of thing and do it well." And she was right. Skelton's test results were recorded, one of the first times a woman's abilities were measured with the same equipment and technology used on men.

Ruth Nichols was another exceptional pilot who had been setting aviation records for decades. The air force invited her to Wright Air Development Center, in Dayton, Ohio, to take some of the astronaut tests and see how she fared. Unlike testing conducted for the *Look* magazine piece, this testing was not for public consumption. But like Skelton, Nichols performed extremely well.

Nichols felt free to speak up for her gender. "I put in a very strong urge that women be used in spaceflights. When I was out at Wright Field, they thought of this with horror, and they said, 'Under no circumstances.'"

The researchers told Nichols that women could not go into space because not enough was known about how they would fare under difficult conditions. To Nichols this just showed that scientists needed to hurry up and focus on testing women. But the air force had no interest in that approach. They were quite content to treat her results as interesting notes to file away and ignore. In fact, when word of how well she had done got out, it soured the whole project.

The air force contact behind Nichols's testing had been Brigadier General Donald Flickinger. Flickinger was a man who was willing to take chances and who shared some of Lovelace's ideas. The two men had been friends for a long time. Flickinger was the one who had suggested Lovelace to NASA for the testing of the Mercury 7 men.

Flickinger got in touch with his old friend.

Lovelace's NASA connections were solidly in place. He knew how to put the astronauts through their paces, and he had a research facility at his disposal.

Flickinger had air force funds.

They put their heads together and named their idea for a female testing program Project WISE (Woman in Space Earliest). In casual conversation, Flickinger often referred to it as a "girl astronaut program." Now all they needed was the perfect test subject.

One of Ruth Nichols's many achievements was helping to organize Relief Wings, which assisted the air force in times of need. Nichols and Amelia Earhart were good friends.

September 1959. Enter Jerrie Cobb.

Slender, with sky-blue eyes, twenty-eight-year-old Jerrie Cobb had been flying airplanes since she was twelve years old. It was in her blood. She had already logged more than 7,000 hours in the air—far more than John Glenn's 5,000 hours and Scott Carpenter's 2,900 hours. She had ferried military aircraft all over the world and set the world altitude record, as well as a world light-plane speed record. And the records she broke were among all pilots—not just women pilots.

All she had ever wanted was to keep going higher, faster, farther.

On this particular morning, she was in Miami, Florida, with her boss, Tom Harris, for the annual Air Force Association meeting.

At seven a.m., they were taking a walk on the beach when two men came out of the surf after their morning swim. Harris recognized them and waved them over. Jerrie didn't know them on sight, but she certainly knew their names when she heard them: Donald Flickinger and Randy Lovelace.

Everyone in aviation knew that Flickinger had his hand in the future of human spaceflight and that Lovelace had worked with the NASA astronauts.

Flickinger and Lovelace hadn't heard of Jerrie Cobb. But here was a world-record–setting, award-winning, *ponytailed* pilot. They were immediately intrigued.

This was the woman they were waiting for. The perfect test subject, standing right in front of them on the beach.

Was it luck? Being in the right place at the right time? That was part of it. But mostly, they got the impression that Jerrie Cobb might just have the Right Stuff.

They invited her back to the Fontainebleau Hotel to talk.

They asked her if there were other young, physically fit female pilots.

They told her that medical tests had shown that women withstand isolation and pain better than men do. But there was no data to show how women would hold up in space-fitness testing.

They wanted those data.

Cobb got a chill up the back of her neck.

Here were men with air force and NASA affiliations wanting to know if she would be their first subject for female astronaut testing. Would she like to volunteer to show how women might fare in space? Would she like to help give women the chance to prove their worth?

Jerrie had had plenty of experience dealing with discrimination in aviation. As a pilot looking for work, she had been told flat out, "No airline passenger will ever fly

When Jerrie Cobb met Randy Lovelace, she was already a record-breaking pilot.

with a woman in the cockpit." Even her father, who supported her desire to be a pilot, had told her, "Honey, it's no career for a woman. . . . A girl doesn't have a chance." The male pilots always got hired first and got the best flying jobs. She was often stuck with the lower-paying jobs the guys didn't want.

She didn't care. She belonged in the air.

And there, standing right in front of her, were men who might just have the power to turn her wildest dreams of flight into reality.

Cobb's eyes filled with tears. She didn't waste a breath. "I jumped at the offer," she said later.

For a while, things went as planned. Flickinger, Lovelace, and Cobb worked together to identify female pilots who would qualify as testing subjects.

But trouble lay ahead.

Flickinger's superiors at the air force were still ruffled about the Ruth Nichols incident. The release of her information to the public implied that the air force was in favor of testing females, which they were not. They told Flickinger that they did not want to conduct any further testing of women for spaceflight.

Flickinger sent Cobb a letter of apology. Project WISE was over. But neither Flickinger nor Lovelace, nor especially Cobb, let that stop them.

Flickinger encouraged Lovelace to proceed without him, and Lovelace put his own foundation behind the project. The idea was to keep their activities quiet until they had enough data to present a solid and convincing case to NASA. The space race pitted American science, medicine, and technology against the science, medicine, and technology of the Russians. It was—or was supposed to be—a contest in which reason, objectivity, tests, and measurements would rule. So if Lovelace could run impeccable tests and come up with unquestionable results, NASA would have to listen.

Lovelace gave Cobb a directive: Don't tell anyone what they were doing until the time was right. This was in keeping with how he handled the Mercury 7 testing. He didn't like to show his hand until he was ready.

He also told her to start training. She was going to need it.

Cobb got moving, making sure she was in her best physical shape for testing. Every morning, she was up at five a.m. and out the door, running laps in her bare feet around the vacant lot next to her house. Then it was off to work. The laps started up again when her workday ended. So did stints on a stationary bicycle. She ran five miles a day and rode twenty miles a day on the bike.

Extra sleep was on the schedule, too, as was lots of protein—steak and hamburgers became regulars on her breakfast menu.

And then the day arrived. Five months after that fateful meeting on the beach, Cobb got word to report to the Lovelace Clinic, in Albuquerque, New Mexico. It was time to prove that women were up to the job.

Failure was not an option.

If she failed, they might never test another woman.

NASA might never get a persuasive report from an influential member of their team filled with data making the case for women as astronaut candidates.

The pressure was on.

February 14, 1960

Astronaut testing, phase one.

In secret, Jerrie Cobb traveled to New Mexico—not to her parents' home for a visit, as coworkers were told.

In secret, she became the first.

The first woman to have the blood tests. And X-rays—more than a hundred. The first to blow into a tube to test her lungs. Jerrie later wrote: "It's the lung-power equivalent of showing muscle strength by hitting a sledgehammer on a scale."

The first to have freezing water injected into her ears. This test froze the inner ear bone, which induces vertigo—a particularly dangerous sensation for pilots because this extreme dizziness completely destroys one's sense of balance and orientation. When the water hit her inner ear, Jerrie's hand fell off the chair arm and she couldn't lift it back up. She went into a whirl. They timed her to see how long it took for her eyeballs to stop spinning, for her to come out of vertigo. The pain of that test was bad. But not nearly as bad as the dread of watching the syringe coming back for more, to repeat the horrendous test on her other ear.

The first to have three feet of rubber hose snaked down her throat. To drink radioactive water.

The first to have probes poke her head to record her brain waves. To give herself an enema before bed. Another upon waking.

The first to take the bike test, pedaling until the point of exhaustion. She knew she would keep going until they told her to stop.

The first to be rocked back and forth, back and forth, on a tilt table, having her heart rate and blood pressure measured every few minutes. Many people pass out during this test. Cobb didn't even get dizzy.

The first to be flown to a secret government location in the mountains of Los Alamos and be slid inside the belly of a machine that measured the amount of radiation in her body.

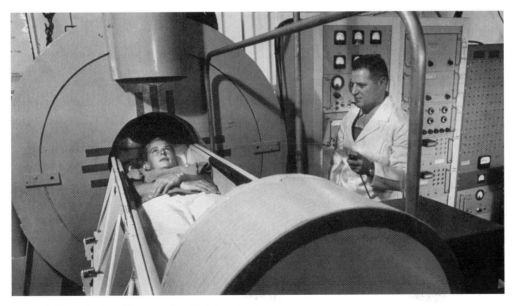

Jerrie Cobb at the Los Alamos scientific laboratory

(Opposite) The Lovelace Clinic in Albuquerque, New Mexico

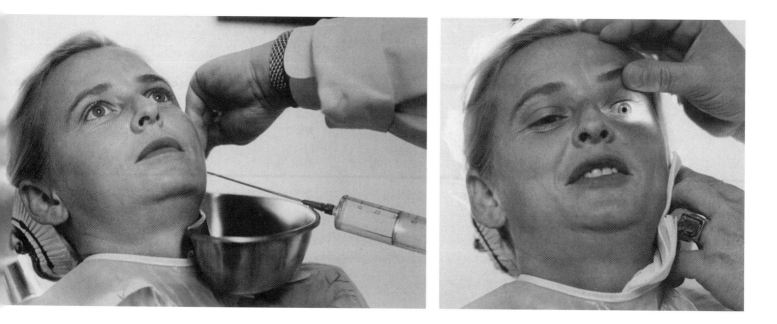

(Left) A syringe full of freezing water is injected into Cobb's inner ear.

(Right) Doctors determine the vertigo effect by examining Cobb's eye.

"Here's the chicken switch," a technician told her. It was pointed out in case panic came over her and she needed to get out. Any chance she'd flip it? None.

The first to be peppered with psychological questions designed to prod her, annoy her, make her angry and lose her cool. One hundred and ninety-five questions, to be exact.

Questions like: What's your favorite hobby? Why? That doesn't seem like a worthwhile activity—why would you want to waste your time doing that?

Questions designed to provoke.

Questions designed to rattle.

Questions like: Do you wish you were dead and away from it all?

Jerrie never lost her cool. Not once.

In secret, she was the first woman to take all eighty-seven of the physical tests the Mercury 7 men had taken.

The first woman to be told that she had passed the Mercury astronaut tests—and, the doctors added, with fewer complaints than the guys.

The first to open the door for others to walk through.

When Jerrie was little, she had to endure a painful doctor's visit to clip the membrane of her tongue. She was reminded of that time during her tests and later reflected, "At five, I'd been given soda pop as a reward. This time I was hoping for something far, far greater."

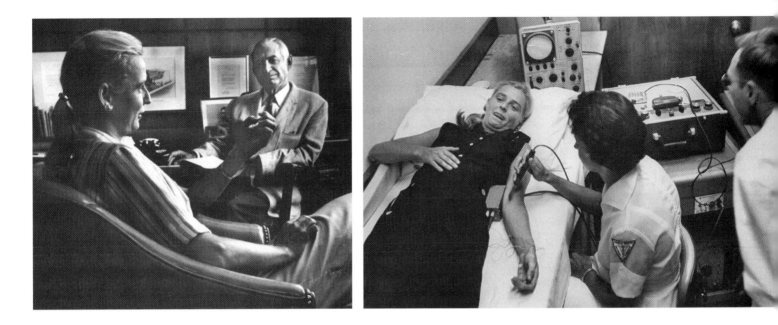

August 19, 1960

Lovelace was at an international space conference in Stockholm and he was ready to make his surprise announcement.

Jerrie had been told to lie low until two things happened—until he made his Stockholm speech and until the August 28 issue of *Life* magazine hit the newsstands, complete with an article and photos about her phase-one testing.

Lovelace delivered his news, telling the world about Cobb's outstanding test results. She had "successfully completed the tests given to the seven men in the United States man-in-space project." He added, "We are already in a position to say that certain qualities of the female space pilot are preferable to those of her male colleague." He also disclosed that "no definite space project [exists] for the women."

Back in New York, where Jerrie Cobb was staying, it was the middle of the night.

Her phone started ringing. Her parents' phone started ringing. Her friends' and colleagues' phones started ringing. And they didn't stop. The world wanted to know who this woman was.

By the next morning, the news was all over the papers. So was her photograph. Shy, soft-spoken Jerrie Cobb was smack in the middle of a media frenzy. Later, she said she felt as if she headed the FBI's "most wanted" list.

Life magazine and *Sports Illustrated* both ran features on her the following week. The *Life* article was particularly powerful, chock-full of photographs of Jerrie hooked

(Left) Randy Lovelace discusses the testing with Jerrie Cobb.

(Right) Cobb is poked and prodded.

up to machines and instruments. People could see, with their own eyes, a woman being tested in exactly the same ways the Mercury 7 had been—taking all the Project Mercury tests—and excelling.

Some cheered her on. Others complimented Cobb but couldn't resist taking jabs. The *Los Angeles Times:* "The scientists haven't even figured out how to get a man to the moon yet, but already they've opened the trip to women. That shows how far the craftier sex has come." Headlines such as MOON MAID'S READY, NO. 1 SPACE GAL SEEMS A LITTLE ASTRONAUGHTY, and 20 YEARS A PILOT, WANTS TO BE AN "ASTRONETTE" all made light of the situation.

Editorial cartoons poked fun.

Reporters included her physical measurements alongside her test results.

Or they dropped the test results completely, asking her what kind of meals she liked to cook and marveling at how slim, blond, and dimpled a pilot could be. "[That] has nothing to do with flying. I never read about men pilots who had their measurements listed in stories about them," Cobb later said.

Consider this unidentified reporter's approach as he interviewed Jerrie Cobb on camera at the time. He seemed unable to separate Cobb from the social stereotype that women should really have only marriage on their mind.

> **Reporter:** *Do you think you can compete with men?*
> **JC:** *I'm not competing with the men at all. I think that both men and women will be flying in space.*
> **Reporter:** *A pretty girl like you must have thought something about marriage—what about that?*
> **JC:** *No, I'm more interested in this right now than anything else in the world.*
> **Reporter:** *You mean that you're a little bit more afraid of men than you are of space?*
> **JC:** *[Uncomfortable laughter] No, I wouldn't say that.*

NASA was not convinced. They were not even interested. The organization announced that it "has never had a plan to put a woman into space, it doesn't have one today, and it doesn't expect to have any in the foreseeable future."

But why? Flickinger commented on why the air force didn't want to continue testing women: "The consensus of opinion . . . was that there was too little to learn of

This cartoon by Jim Lange is from the August 20, 1960, edition of Cobb's hometown newspaper, the *Daily Oklahoman*.

value." There was also the issue of the physiological differences between men and women, which seemed to make space researchers squirm. Although men like Flickinger and Lovelace knew better, there were others who believed in the mythology that a woman's menstruation cycle affected her brain. This belief was so prevalent among doctors during World War II that women who served as WASP routinely answered the question "How often do you get your period?" with "I am highly irregular" to keep from being restricted from flying. The absurd fear was that women were more likely to crash their planes during their cycle. Even in 1960, many researchers still believed in this medical myth.

Apparently, women's bodies posed yet another problem. Some claimed it would take too much time and cost too much money to redesign pressure suits for them. Flickinger told Lovelace, "One of the major objections made . . . was that we could not justify the expense of altering the PPSs [partial-pressure suits] to fit the girls."

Lovelace was not deterred by any of this. And the media was embracing Cobb. As far as they were concerned, she was America's first "lady astronaut."

(Opposite) Cobb during the tilt-table test

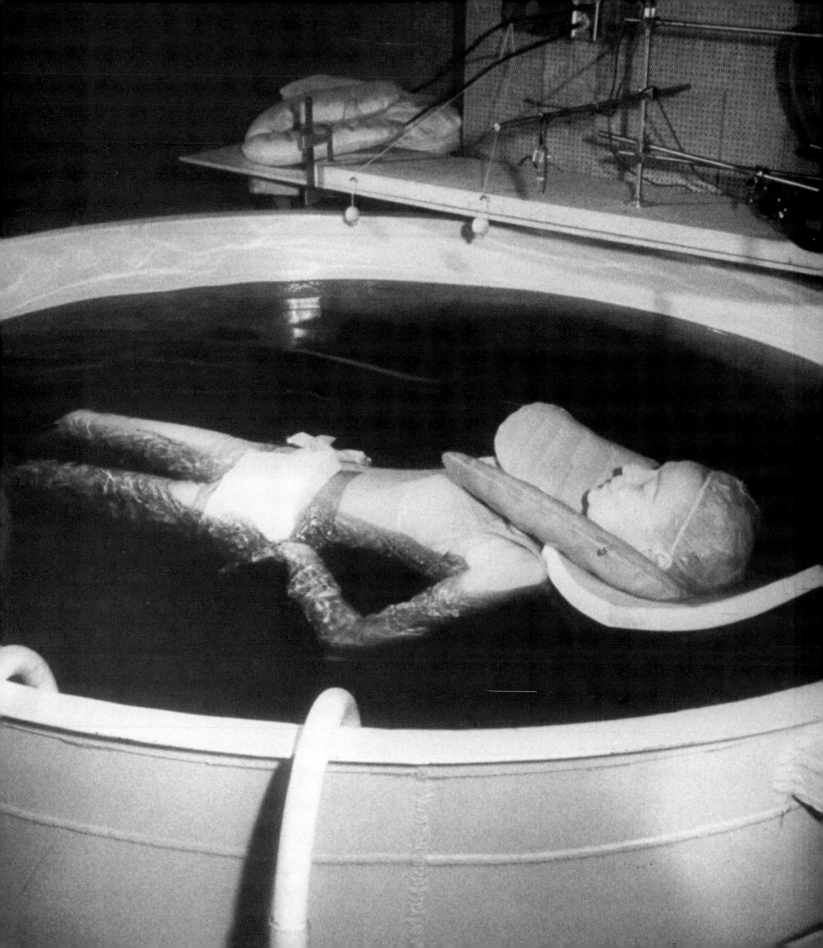

Chapter 3

NOT a Meaningful Test

The Tank

Picture this: *You are surrounded by complete and utter darkness, pitch black. All you can hear is your heart beating, your breath as you inhale, exhale, inhale, exhale. You are floating in a tank of water the exact same temperature as your body. Where does your body end and the water begin?*

A full over-the-head mask with air hoses to breathe through is used with some subjects. But drips of water creeping in could be distracting, and the air line sometimes leaks. You opt for foam pillows around your neck and waist to help keep you afloat.

It is peaceful, quiet, dark.

Your mind drifts.

What did I have for dinner last night?

What was that joke?

Where should I go on vacation?

1, 2, 3, 4, 5, 6, 7, 8, . . . 999, 1000.

My ten favorite movies are . . .

You are bored.

It is too quiet.

Jerrie Cobb floats peacefully in the isolation tank designed to test how well an astronaut might fare in the isolation of space.

You smack your hand on the surface of the water. You cannot feel the splash.

It is too dark.

So dark your eyes cannot adjust. But wait. Is that a sliver of light coming from over there? You think you remember seeing the door there, back before the lights went out.

When was that, exactly?

An hour ago? Two hours? Six?

Is there light coming in under that door or not? It can't be; the room is lightproof. Still, you are sure you see it. Light, creeping in, flickering, teasing your brain.

You smell hamburgers cooking on a grill. Impossible. The eight-inch walls make the room smellproof, too.

Are you hallucinating? The thought makes your breath come faster. You speak, simply to hear more sound.

"How long have I been in here?"

No reply.

Don't panic. You remember now, they told you no one would answer you.

Relax.

You reassure yourself that nothing in this room can harm you. You are in no danger; you are here of your own free will. You inspected the tank yourself. Saw that it was round and deep and contained nothing but water.

Nothing.

"I need to get out!"

The lights flip on and a scientist comes into the room to help you out of the isolation tank. You ask how long you were in and are asked to estimate.

"About eight hours?"

It has been only three.

These were the feelings many people who participated in Dr. Jay Shurley's isolation-tank testing experienced. At first, they found the floating sensation peaceful. They meditated. They enjoyed the silence. But more than half would then begin to have hallucinations—seeing, hearing, and smelling things that were not there. Voices talking to them, lights flashing, the smoky odor of burning toast. One man saw a giant frog, an ocean liner, and a larger-than-life man looking down on him. Some people would sing or be overwhelmed by childhood memories and start to cry. Others would talk incessantly about the people in their lives or moments that bothered them or surprised them or made them happy, sad, or angry. Some ticked off grocery lists. Anything to pass the time, *mark* the time, in whatever way they could.

Isolation testing was considered important from the beginning of the space program, since being in space is probably the most challenging form of isolation a human being will ever encounter. Being sealed up in a space capsule thousands of miles from Earth could trigger a panic attack. And having a panic attack in space is not like having a panic attack at your desk—you could die, and destroy millions of dollars' worth of equipment in the process. But none of the Mercury 7 men went through the water-tank isolation testing, which was much more rigorous than the simpler isolation test the men took in an empty room.

One reporter asked Shurley if he could give the tank a go, in order to write a story about it. For thirty minutes, he was calm and quiet. But for the next four hours, he couldn't keep his mouth shut. He babbled. He sang. He heard a dog barking. He had a fit of hysterical laughter. He whistled to keep up his courage. He saw copper-colored coins that weren't there. He acted as though he were drunk, talking to a voice he believed he heard talking to him. He said, "I didn't know it was possible to be so alone." Finally, he said he was bored and climbed out. "I honestly believe, if you put a person in there, just kept him and fed him by vein, he'd just flat out die!"

September 1960

Now it was Cobb's turn to tackle the tank.

She had had a good night's sleep. She felt ready to be alone with herself.

Down, down, down to the basement she went.

Once alone in the tank room, she settled in to the water. It was slightly salty, which made it easier for her to float. A gentle swirl of circulation filtered the water, eliminating the need for bathroom breaks.

"All set," she said.

The microphone hanging just above the water's surface alerted Shurley's graduate assistant Cathryn Walters, who was monitoring her every word next door.

The room went dark.

Cobb knew how many people had cracked in the isolation tank. She promised herself that she would not be one of them.

Cobb was quiet.

Cobb was still.

Two hours passed.

"Just reporting in that everything's fine."

Four hours.

"I find the less I move, the more I like it."

She did not chatter. She did not splash.

All was still. Quiet. Near weightless.

She wondered if this was what it was like in space and when she would find out.

Six and a half hours. Cobb had now been in the tank longer than anyone.

Would her stubborn calm break soon?

Eight hours.

"Everything's fine . . . very peaceful."

She thought she saw a light but knew that was impossible. Still, she had agreed to report what she saw or felt.

"There's some light coming in on the floor, probably by the door."

She thought this was probably one of those hallucinations they had told her about.

More time passed.

"Reporting in again: everything's fine . . . very peaceful."

Still more time went by.

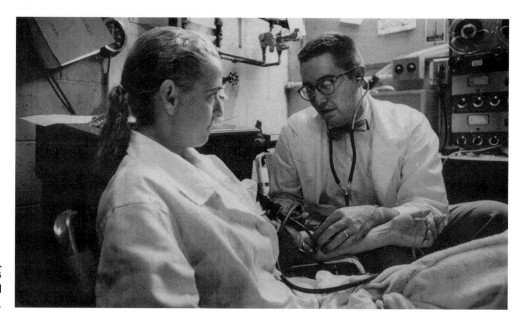

Dr. Jay Shurley examines Cobb after she has emerged from the water isolation tank.

Finally she told Walters, "I think I'll get out of the tank unless you want me to stay in longer."

She got the OK and climbed out.

When the lights came up, Walters discovered a tiny gap in the wall where the air supply poked through. Cobb hadn't imagined the light after all.

She later reported that her mind had wandered in the tank. She thought about her sister and the little dachshund, Schatzi, she had had as a child. But she kept it to herself in the tank. She wanted to surpass all expectations.

And she did.

When asked to guess what time it was, Cobb estimated: "Two or two thirty p.m."

It was seven o'clock at night. She had shattered all previous records.

Nine hours and forty minutes.

Shurley said, "Probably not one in one thousand persons would be capable of making such a lengthy isolation run. . . . Extraordinary."

I Enjoy Reading *Mechanics Monthly*

So, hypothetically, if one thousand people were to attempt an isolation run, how might the men fare in comparison to the women? In the late 1950s and '60s, men were generally regarded as the levelheaded ones. They were the ones who could be counted on to keep their cool, handle a sticky situation, rescue a damsel in distress. Television, books, magazines, comics, all showed manly men tackling life head-on. Marlboro Man cigarette commercials were punctuated by the theme song of the action-packed Western *The Magnificent Seven* for a double shot of testosterone, and the Hollywood star John Wayne was the ultimate macho icon—often playing strong, reliable, soft-spoken but tough cowboys or soldiers on the big screen.

What about the women? Have you ever seen reruns on late-night TV of shows from the late '50s and early '60s? On *The Dick Van Dyke Show*, Rob Petrie's pretty, smart (but never *too* smart) wife, Laura, is most likely to be heard sobbing the words, "Oh, Rooooobbb" in a moment of stress, because on her own she can rarely find a solution to whatever problem arises. June Cleaver, mother of the "Beave" on *Leave It to Beaver*, wouldn't have been caught dead contradicting her husband and would always defer to his best judgment, much like the mother in another popular show of the time, *Father Knows Best*. The title says it all.

Television shows of the time did not portray women as powerful figures. (Top) Lucille Ball as Lucy Ricardo, the lovable screw-up in *I Love Lucy*. (Left) Laura Petrie's husband, Rob, was always there to save the day on *The Dick Van Dyke Show*. (Right) The classic roles of a stereotypical 1950s family were played out on *Father Knows Best*.

Lucy Ricardo was the ultimate dizzy chick in *I Love Lucy*, married to slick, smooth Ricky Ricardo. It was always Lucy causing the trouble, Lucy making an ever-increasing mess of things—however lovable and hilarious she was—and Ricky saving the day. Advertisements portrayed women as the authority on topics such as knowing exactly which dish detergent would keep their hands softest and which coffeemaker would allow them to make that perfect cup of coffee.

But even as these images were reinforcing the idea that men were more capable of handling stress than women, Shurley and Walters were proving otherwise. They wanted to challenge these stories about men and women with hard facts. One way to do this was to compare the results of Cobb's tank test to the results of the isolation tests the Mercury 7 men took—which Shurley did not even believe were tough enough to be meaningful.

All the Mercury 7 men had to do was spend a two- to three-hour stint in a dark room that was equipped with a desk, chair, pad of paper, and pen. How hard could that really be? John Glenn simply felt his way around the room until he discovered the desk and paper, then wrote down his thoughts to pass the time. Shurley had assisted with the Mercury 7 testing. When the results were sent to him, he wrote across the top, *NOT a meaningful test!* There was no weightlessness involved to simulate space. And the men had something to do with their time—write.

Long after Cobb climbed into the tank, studies showed that men need external stimuli (pen and paper, in this case) in order to cope with stress, while women do not. This may well mean that female astronauts are better equipped to handle the stresses of space. But at the time, few scientists were willing to see Cobb's results as any kind of challenge to the dominant ideas about the capabilities of men and women. Only recently have objective tests challenged those ancient beliefs. In 1961, NASA doctors admitted that the men's test was limited but said that they felt it was good enough to tell whether any of the astronauts would become agitated in space.

In fact, Cobb's test showed not only that she wouldn't become agitated; it suggested that she would *excel* in space. Jerrie Cobb's performance made the Mercury 7's isolation testing look like a walk in the park. Shurley estimated that spending fifteen minutes in his water tank was the equivalent of spending two days in the isolation room the men used. Cobb, Shurley determined, was psychologically fit for space.

But the isolation tank wasn't the only way Shurley and Walters had tested Cobb's psyche.

Before she ever went into the tank, she went through in-depth psychological testing. She had an IQ test, anxiety tests, the Rorschach test, and took the MMPI test, a series of questions designed to analyze the testee's personality and screen for psychological disorders.

I enjoy reading *Mechanics Monthly.*	Circle TRUE or FALSE.
I have planned a party for 20 people.	Circle TRUE or FALSE.
Swimming is relaxing.	Circle TRUE or FALSE.

Just this one test includes 558 additional questions.

Her answers were analyzed.

There were splotches of ink on paper. What, she was asked, did she see?

Her answers were analyzed.

There were sentences to complete:

I like to read because _____ .

People dance to _____ .

My mother is sad when _____ .

Her answers were analyzed.

She was asked about her childhood. Her teenage years. How she felt about work.

Her answers were analyzed.

They hooked electrodes to her head and measured brain activity while she was awake. And while she was asleep.

She was asked to speak nonstop for five full minutes about herself.

Now, *that* Cobb could have done without.

Thirty hours later, she had her phase-two results. Once again, Cobb had excelled. Proven she had the Right Stuff.

And once again, her attitude was noted as being more impressive than that of the Mercury 7 men, who balked at the psychological questions and grew irritated. They didn't like answering them and said so. Jerrie never complained.

Cobb was not about to stop with a few tests. She wanted to face everything that had been thrown at the men. So she asked NASA for permission to take the MASTIF for a spin. This time, she got lucky. Someone there said yes.

MASTIF

The MASTIF, or multiple-axis space test inertia facility, was a huge gyroscope—as big as a house—consisting of three aluminum cages laced together. The contraption was designed to pitch up and down, lurch side to side, and even spin in circles. That way, a pilot could experience what it was like to be in a spacecraft in trouble, out of control. And the scientists monitoring the pilot could see how he—and now, she—would react, how quickly they could operate the controls to bring the machine level.

When Mercury 7 astronaut Alan Shepard first faced the MASTIF, he went "green and pressed the red 'chicken switch.'"

Cobb was no chicken.

She climbed up into the enormous metal machine.

A mock space-capsule seat waited for her in the inner cage. The scientists strapped her in. Seat belt. Helmet. Chest harness. Leg restraints.

Imagine every roller-coaster ride you've ever taken. Now imagine one ride that combines every stomach-churning moment of them all. The MASTIF was about to spin and twist and pitch Cobb. This would show how much she could take, how quickly she could tame the beast.

You had to have a gentle touch. If you moved the controls too much or not enough, you could make things worse and spiral out of control.

"Are you ready?" they asked.

"Yes."

The MASTIF began to move. First one cage, then the second, then the third. Soon Cobb was "twisting like a top, and going head-over-heels at the same time." Her vision "was a dizzying blur."

Cobb fought the nausea. She focused her vision.

She took charge of the joystick.

Move by move, she brought each rotating axis under control.

Cobb mastered the MASTIF. Mercury-style.

(Left) Jerrie Cobb masters the multiple-axis space test inertia facility, or MASTIF. (Right) A full-scale view of the MASTIF.

Chapter 4

Mommy's Going to the Moon!

An Invitation to the Party

Some women were following Cobb's story with more than a passing interest.

"When I was twenty-one, I saw Jerrie Cobb in *Life* magazine, training to be an astronaut, and said, 'Whoa, I've got to do that.'" Wally Funk sat down and wrote a letter to Lovelace. It got her a well-deserved invitation to join the party. Funk was a flying instructor and already had 3,000 hours in the air.

Myrtle "K" Cagle learned about Lovelace's program in a similar way. "There was an article in the Sunday paper saying the recruiting was on, so I wrote to them." She, too, qualified as a candidate. Cagle was also a flight instructor, with 4,300 flying hours to her name.

The world of female pilots was a small one. Word of mouth was almost as swift as the media.

Gene Nora Stumbough—another female flight instructor with an impressive record—heard about Lovelace's program from Wally Funk at an air race. "So, I wrote Dr. Lovelace and I basically told him that I just didn't see how he could do this program without me." But Stumbough did not read too much into things. "I was never told that we were in contention for an astronaut slot. I knew it was the same physical test the astronauts took—but that's all."

In 1957, Jean Hixson became the fourth woman to break the sound barrier.

Myrtle "K" Cagle was a newlywed when she got the call to try out for Lovelace's program.

Since the first planning stages, Lovelace had been gathering the names of exceptional female pilots. Now letters went out to them, inviting them to take the same tests Cobb had mastered.

Marion Dietrich received such a letter.

Will you volunteer for the initial examinations for woman astronaut candidate? it read.

"I stumbled to a chair and fell into it," Dietrich later reported in an article for *McCalls,* a magazine aimed at women. "In stunned disbelief, I reread the letter's first paragraph and began the second: 'The examinations take one week and are done on a purely voluntary basis. They do not commit you to any further part of the Woman in Space Program unless you so desire.'"

The letter was signed, *Dr. W. Randolph Lovelace II, Director of the Lovelace Foundation.*

Marion's twin sister, Jan, received a similar letter.

Both were experienced fliers. Jan was a working pilot and an instructor; Marion was a reporter who flew whenever she had the chance.

Fly Girls

All told, eighteen women were willing and able to face the challenges Cobb had faced. (See full list on page 122.)

It was time for the rest of phase one to begin.

All these women shared Cobb's passion for flying. All were accomplished professional pilots. All had made flying lives for themselves.

This was no small feat in a field filled with men. They had worked hard—and some had had to talk fast—to wrangle the jobs they had. Some transported cargo in airplanes. Several had airline-transport ratings, the highest rank in general aviation—a rarity for women. In fact, in 1960, only 21 out of all 3,246 female pilots in the country had this rating. Irene Leverton was also one of the few female agricultural pilots in the country, dusting crops in four states.

Some had aircraft-maintenance licenses—they worked on the airplanes—which was very unusual. Some were test pilots. Some flew air taxis, or taught flying lessons, or both. B Steadman even had her own flight school.

All the women had experienced discrimination and prejudice and had learned to work around it. And there were certainly people who had adapted to the idea of female pilots. Rhea Hurrle spent some time flying hunters and fishermen into the woods. "Passengers might be nervous, but not after they'd flown with me. After that, most of them requested me as their pilot."

Some of the other women were not as lucky. When faced with bias against female pilots, they tried to fight back and lost out on jobs. Others learned to lower their expectations, accepting jobs flying smaller planes, or taking fewer flights, or ferrying cargo when they were qualified to carry passengers.

They all learned to be sure they looked like "ladies"—feminine, well dressed, polished.

In a society where women were to have dinner on the table at six p.m. for their husbands returning home from work, it was bad enough that they had the nerve to be women earning a living. Worse, it was in such an unladylike field as aviation. If they didn't wear skirts while climbing in and out of their cockpits, powder their noses, and freshen their lipstick, they risked jeers and jokes from some of their male peers.

And in order to work in aviation, there was one more thing they needed to do: keep any ideas they had about women's rights to themselves. Being a lone woman looking for a flying job was hard enough. If you were seen as a woman who wanted to have the same opportunities as a man, you were labeled a troublemaker, and you didn't have a chance.

The Dietrich twins learned to fly together as teenagers.

The youngest of the group, Wally Funk was only twenty-one when she volunteered for the Lovelace program.

Testing participant Irene Leverton remembers that well. "See, if the word got out that you were really a feminist, you couldn't get a job anywhere. So it was a matter of doing the best you could, being quiet, and then if it got too bad, you told them off and quit. But if you made big public things all the time, you were dead. You were going to starve."

For Women Only

Now, finally, all these fantastic female pilots who shared the dream of flight were about to share a new dream—the dream of *spaceflight*.

From January through August 1961, the women went for testing. First stop: the dingy, dirty "ratty-looking" Bird of Paradise Motel, across the street from the Lovelace Clinic. They arrived in ones and twos. Ready to "be up at 5:30 or 6:00 . . . running all day long." They put everything on hold—husbands, children, jobs—for this chance. It wasn't easy to get away. They were working women, mothers, wives.

Jerri Sloan greets her young son.

Sarah Gorelick got word by phone just one day before Lovelace needed her to show up. She was in Kansas City, working as an engineer, but she managed to get the time off she needed and went to the clinic.

Jane Hart took a break from many responsibilities—including flying President John F. Kennedy's mother, Rose, around in Hart's airplane marked FOR WOMEN ONLY—and hightailed it to the grocery store. She filled three carts so she could stock her fridge with enough food to feed her eight kids while she was gone.

Jerri Sloan read her letter from Lovelace to her nine-year-old son. When she got to the part that said "volunteering for the initial examinations for female astronaut candidates," he didn't wait to hear the rest. He was out the door, hollering, "Mommy's going to the moon!"

Some had support right off the bat. The boss of former WASP and schoolteacher Jean Hixson was on board, no problem. Others needed to persuade their bosses to grant them time off. Some did so at the risk of losing their jobs while they were away.

Some of the women were criticized for taking on "unnatural" roles. Doubters questioned their devotion to their children and husbands. Jane Hart's husband, a U.S. senator, received bags of mail from constituents who thought it disgraceful that his wife was flying all over creation and told him he should exercise more control over her.

You Want an Astronaut, by God, I'll Give You One

It didn't matter what other people thought. These were women who knew their own minds, their own hearts, their own dreams.

They showed up ready for anything: to be run ragged, spun in circles, pushed to their limits. They were ready to show their smarts, their strength, their courage. They were determined to show what they already knew—that the Boys Club needed to let in the Girls, that they were up to the job.

They all knew what was at stake. Stumbough later said, "You were carrying everybody else on your shoulders."

The manager at the Bird of Paradise tried to rattle some of the women as they checked in. To Marion Dietrich he said ominously, "You're really in for it. It's rough. Why, the girls today, they were like to quit, but I talked them into stayin'. Talked the ones last week into stayin', too."

Marion Dietrich had had a bit of a heads-up because her sister Jan went first and sent her letters with tips. "Come with a little extra weight; you miss one or two meals every day." And, "Try not to have your color portrait taken the day they rub clay all over your head for the electroencephalogram." Jan got to the heart of the challenge that all the women faced when she told her sister to "combine a saint-like discipline with an unholy determination."

If women were going to prove they could equal the best of men—the chosen Mercury 7—they would have to show not only that they were as tough or tougher, but that they could do it with a smile, never stepping out of the role of the polite, cooperative lady. As the saying goes, the great dancer and movie star Ginger Rogers was just as talented as her partner Fred Astaire—except that she did all the steps backward and in high heels. In effect, Cobb and the women who followed her were being asked to perform just as well as the Mercury 7 but backward and in high heels.

Gene Nora Stumbough and Jane Hart met for the first time at the Bird of Paradise.

Hart had a good sense of humor, which helped them both. When Hart saw a photo of bones in a dish, she told Stumbough, "Well, here we are, Gene Nora—this is us now, and *this* is us after we get through this thing."

Jerri Sloan and B Steadman also met for the first time at the Bird of Paradise. Each day, the women faced the grueling tests alone. But each night, on the porch of their motel, they met for their "Lovelace cocktail hour" and compared notes. One evening they had a laughing fit while imagining the Mercury 7 heroes dealing with the same messy daily enemas they had to handle.

Examinations took all day. There was an eye exam that lasted more than four hours. There were pain tolerance tests, including one in which testees held one hand in ice water for several minutes while having their blood pressure measured, then did it all over again with the other hand. It felt like "a million needles were sticking into the arm and hand," B Steadman said.

One of the tests involved riding a stationary bike. What's the big deal? one might wonder. Any kid can do that. For one thing, it came after a grueling morning of other tests, a morning when testees had had no breakfast and only a light lunch. For

B Steadman (left) and Jane Hart

another, they rode with their face pushed tight against a plastic mouthpiece connected to a tube of air and were hooked up to an array of monitors so white-coated scientists could check their heart rate, blood pressure, and stamina. And all the while they had to keep pace to a metronome *click-click-click*ing away as they went, had to avoid missing a beat or slowing down whenever the incline was made steeper, had to avoid showing any signs of weakness until the scientists were satisfied and said they could stop.

Other tests involved more poking and prodding. Blood tests were done. Body fluids were examined. Tubes went in and tubes went out, up, down, and around. X-rays were taken. When there was pain involved, none of these women showed it.

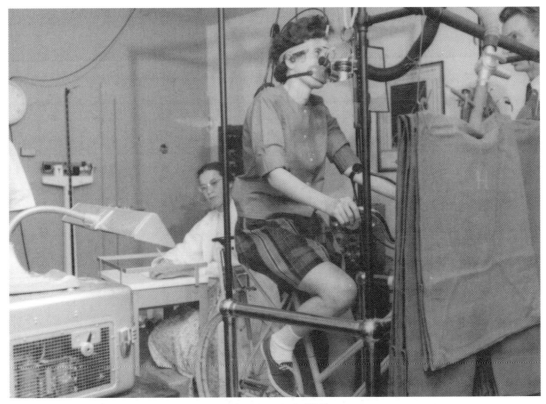

Gene Nora Stumbough takes the bicycle test at the Lovelace Clinic.

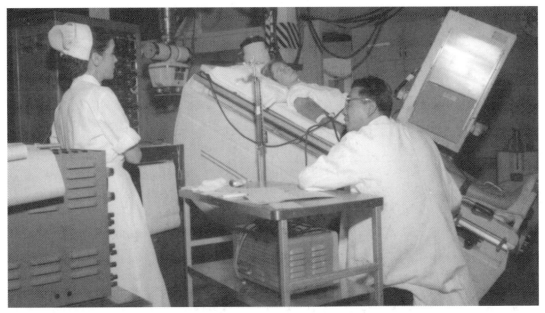

Jane Hart during the tilt-table test at the Lovelace Clinic

Their smiles stayed plastered in place. Teeth gritted, they grinned through the pain. Not one of them would ever complain.

"We never stopped until they told us to stop. We didn't even say ouch and, boy, they hurt us," Jerri Sloan Truhill later remembered. Their determination was fierce. Her attitude said it all: "You want an astronaut, by God, I'll give you one."

Into the Monster

It didn't matter what kind of tests were thrown at them. They were tough. They could take whatever was dished out—even a flight to an unknown location.

Imagine. *You step off a private plane. You don't know exactly where you are, but you know it is top secret. Los Alamos.*

Clearance papers are checked. You are told to follow. You do. Onto an elevator that plummets down, down, down. You walk through dusky hallways, deep in the ground. Finally, you face a set of doors. Big, heavy doors. You enter. The doors thunk closed behind you. In front of you is a tomblike thing. As big as a tanker truck and as round as a barrel. It takes up the whole room.

The only glimpse of its inner workings is a human-size drawer, which is open— ready to carry its next subject—you—into its belly.

You are told to undress, scrub clean, and slip on a white gown. You climb up the wooden steps to the drawer's opening and lie down on cold, hard metal. A body on a stretcher.

You fold your arms across your chest and stay silent.

Perfectly still.

You are about to be slid on a slab into the mouth of the monster: the total-body counter.

When the door shuts, every speck of light is blocked out. It is as dark as the blackest night. Darker.

Then you wait. Completely motionless in this coffin-like contraption while the total-body counter painlessly bombards you with electronic rays and counts the amount of radioactivity in your body. It measures the ratio of muscle to fat in your body, too. If you get claustrophobic or begin to panic, there is a "chicken switch." You won't need it.

Strong Enough, Smart Enough, Fit Enough

When phase-one testing was finished, Lovelace analyzed the results. Of the nineteen women who were put through the tests, thirteen of them—including Cobb—aced every last one. They passed with flying colors.

B Steadman remembered Lovelace saying what he thought would happen next. He believed, she said, that "we collectively had done a good job of showing them what women could do versus what men could do and that there was no reason to exclude us from being accepted by NASA."

He had his data. His theory that women—who were lighter and therefore less expensive for NASA to use—were suitable astronaut candidates was proven right.

The results offered solid scientific evidence that women were not, in fact, the weaker sex. And they had proven to be every bit the risk takers men were.

Now no one could say that women weren't strong enough, or smart enough, or fit enough, to fly into space.

Could they?

As a female pilot, Irene Leverton encountered discrimination on a regular basis.

Well, maybe. Some of the women were fortunate to have supportive people in their lives who were thrilled for them. Others were not so lucky.

Irene Leverton's boss stopped scheduling her for flights and eventually demoted her, taking away her multi-engine privileges. Jerri Sloan's husband greeted her at the airport with divorce papers.

One of the men Marion Dietrich was dating wondered if the women were just being used in a plan to colonize space stations and asked, "Is that what they might use you for?" His conclusion: "Let the scientists dig up their own women."

Another one of her beaus said, "But I was thinking of asking you to marry me." Marion told him to keep on thinking. She knew what her priorities were. She would not be deterred.

None of them would.

Chapter 5

Too Good to Be True

May 1961

While the other woman candidates were being put through their paces at the Lovelace clinic for phase-one testing, Cobb had moved on from the phase-two psychological testing to phase three. Lovelace had been turned down by the air force when he asked to use their facilities but had gotten the go-ahead to put Cobb through testing at the Naval School of Aviation Medicine, in Pensacola, Florida. He also started making inroads for the other twelve to follow in her footsteps.

Cobb arrived on a hot, sticky night and got a good night's sleep. She was going to need it.

Her schedule for the following day looked like it would be even more grueling than in Albuquerque or Oklahoma City.

And it was. She was expected to perform the same fitness drills as the navy pilots, with no allowances made for her weight or size. There were long runs in the humid heat. Sit-ups, which she did fine. Chin-ups, which were hard. And, harder still, trying to climb over a six-and-a-half-foot wall.

The first time she leaped at it, she fell.

No matter. She ran and jumped at the wall again. This time, Cobb clawed her way to the top—and got over.

Jerrie Cobb poses next to a Mercury space capsule.

Jerrie Cobb in the altitude chamber. She is wearing an oversize men's pressure suit because there were no suits made for women.

"Scratched, bruised, and breathless," she later said, but it was worth it—no way would she let a little thing like a wall get in her way.

Then came the airborne electroencephalogram (EEG) test. This would determine her reaction to the pull of gravity during aerobatic maneuvers. She needed permission to fly in the navy's fully loaded Douglas Skyraider. Pensacola wired navy headquarters, in Washington, D.C., to get clearance for Cobb, explaining that it was for a test to examine the differences between male and female astronaut candidates. Permission was granted, but not without the return jab: "If you don't know the difference already, we refuse to put money into the project."

It wasn't a lone opinion. There were men around the base who weren't thrilled to have her there. They were waiting to see if she could cut it. Waiting to watch her fail.

Cobb climbed into the copilot's seat. Eighteen probes were attached to her head, and a camera and other recording devices were hooked up to record her every move.

The pilot made that plane climb, dive, loop, roll, swerve—death-defying feats.

The camera captured the movements beyond her control—eyeballs out, eyeballs in—but fear never crept across her face.

And once she got off the plane, there was more in store for her.

The altitude-chamber check would show how Cobb's body reacted to the low pressure of high altitudes. The higher the altitude, the lower the pressure. A pressure suit adds pressure to the body, keeping the gases in one's blood from coming out in potentially fatal bubbles. And, like Skelton before her, Cobb was buckled and strapped into a way-too-big pressure suit made in men's sizes only.

Testers lowered the pressure in the chamber to what it would be at an altitude of 60,000 feet, when it is hard to move at all, but she did, turning knobs and dials as told, moving arms and legs that felt lead-heavy due to lack of oxygen. Then they suddenly increased the pressure, as though her craft was going into a free fall, plummeting down to 10,000 feet.

Still fine.

Still strong.

Next up: the Dilbert Dunker.

Picture it: *Above a pool, at the top of a steep ramp, is a metal cockpit. You are loaded down—suited up in full flight gear, helmet, parachute. You climb into the contraption and are buckled in. The door clangs shut. The metal cage then hurtles down the ramp, slams into the pool, flips upside down, sinks to the bottom, and fills with water.*

Sixteen feet down.

Will you panic? Will you know which way is up? Which way is down?

Will you be able to get your bearings, extract yourself from the capsule, and swim to safety?

Cobb was ready. She gave a thumbs-up, the signal to let loose. The capsule lurched down the ramp, filling with water. First to her knees, then quickly over her head. It flipped upside down, and plunged to the bottom of the pool. Jerrie held her breath. She knew she could likely hold it for one minute.

She unbuckled. Unhooked. Untangled. Made sure her suit didn't catch on any-thing—a handle here, a knob there. Jerrie later described what she had to do. She was "slowly maneuvering, 'up' toward the top of the capsule, which was 'down' toward the bottom of the pool." She did not get disoriented. She found the hatch and opened it. She was out.

The Dilbert Dunker sequence—the capsule speeds toward the pool (left), hits the water (right), then turns upside down at the bottom of the pool.

Then came the easy part—swimming to the surface. Rescue divers at the ready didn't have to get wet that day.

The Dilbert Dunker was the water survival test. Then came the airborne survival test, which simulated the experience of being in an ejection seat: the testee was sent flying up a steep track before being slammed back down it. And the SRR: the slow-rotation room. A room perched on a centrifuge spins around and around and around—ten times a minute. No windows. No horizon to help you get your bearings.

Inside, when asked to walk, Cobb wobbled. She staggered.

Then she rallied: The dials came into focus. She performed every task asked of her. She was not one of the ones to lose her lunch.

Test after test after test was a success.

Cobb came through it all.

Now that Cobb had passed all the hurdles, Lovelace was ready to continue testing the other twelve women. Their time would come in July. He and Cobb wanted to get the women to Pensacola before any of the top brass could change their minds about the whole thing. Cobb sent each woman a letter addressed *Dear F.L.A.T. (fellow lady astronaut trainee)*.

Cobb on Center Stage

Before May was out, Cobb was back in her home state of Oklahoma for the First National Conference on the Peaceful Uses of Space. Lovelace was there, too, as were NASA officials, politicians, scientists in the field of space research and travel, and the press.

It was the perfect opportunity for Lovelace to stir up excitement about Cobb's results, as well as unveil his big idea.

This time his news wasn't about just one woman. This time, he revealed that other women had also completed phase one with outstanding results. Other women were waiting in the wings to continue along Cobb's path.

The news caused a commotion. Quiet Cobb was back on center stage.

That night at the banquet, she was put at the head table, right next to James Webb, NASA's administrator. He was the guest speaker for the evening. Cobb knew exactly who she was seated next to. She had already written to him to report her testing accomplishments and to point out Russia's intent to send a woman into space.

Cobb noticed Webb scribbling notes on his speech all during dinner. When he stood to speak, he was armed with a little surprise announcement of his own.

Webb named Cobb a special NASA consultant in manned spaceflight.

Cobb was thrilled, and surprised. She posed for photographers next to a mock-up of a Mercury capsule. "I was actually to have a say in America's move into space! It was too good to be true."

Why did Webb do it? Did he really need her? More likely, it was a smart public-relations move. With a female consultant on the job, NASA would be above criticism. Organizations do not like to be told that they are wrong, that they have left out qualified people, that they need to change.

Cobb was quietly sworn in for her new assignment. No fanfare. When reporters wanted details about her responsibilities, Webb did not have them. He simply said that she would be "a great asset to any part of the program."

Cobb set right to work drafting a proposal to have NASA utilize women in the space program. The first part "recommended that research be continued officially, by NASA." The second part made the formal request that America beat the Russians in putting the first woman in space.

She waited for a reply.

Early July 1961

There were problems with the upcoming July testing date at Pensacola. Scheduling conflicts. Lovelace and the navy worked out a new date, in September.

Cobb was worried. She didn't like the loss of momentum. To make up for it, she suggested to the women that anyone who could, should come to Oklahoma and take the psychological tests.

Late July 1961

Rhea Hurrle has a beautiful smile. A warm spirit with a no-nonsense air. She didn't tell a single soul about the testing she went through in March—not even her family. They didn't find out for two more years, when a *Life* magazine article profiled all thirteen of the women.

But that July, she had two people she could talk to: Jerrie Cobb and Wally Funk. The three of them were at Cobb's home in Oklahoma City. Having a cookout in the backyard. Seeing who could do the most sit-ups. Laughing.

Rhea Hurrle smiles from the cockpit of her plane.

Funk would begin phase-two isolation testing in the morning.

A few days earlier, Hurrle had arrived to do the same. She borrowed a Piper Comanche airplane from her boss and flew herself there from Texas. Cobb gave her a warm welcome, putting her up at her house. She even had fun decorating the guest room for the occasion. At the time, one of the most popular TV shows was a Western called *Have Gun, Will Travel.* Cobb hung a banner that read *Have Urge, Will Orbit.* She dotted the ceiling with stars and planets and bought new bedspreads with spaceships on them.

Hurrle reported to the same place Cobb had: the isolation chamber in Shurley's laboratory, located in the Veterans Administration hospital in Oklahoma City.

She later remembered the experience as relaxing. "If you kept your wits about you, it was fine. But I guess some people couldn't quite handle it. I stayed in until they told me to come out."

She did indeed. Breaking Cobb's record. Hurrle stayed in the tank a full ten hours—twenty minutes longer than Cobb. Her movement during that whole time was recorded as "very minimal," and she spoke little.

Then it was Funk's turn.

Earplugs in, and off she went—into the pitch-black tank. No sound, no light—no problem.

She barely moved or spoke.

Funk did even better than Hurrle: ten hours and thirty-five minutes. In fact, she climbed out only because Walters asked her to—and she was fine. She said she could have stayed in indefinitely.

As the summer came to a close, the last woman—Jean Hixson—completed phase one, and all the signed release letters arrived in Cobb's mailbox.

But still no word from NASA. No response to her proposal.

No consulting for the consultant to do.

The silence was ominous.

AKRON BEACON JOURNAL

PARADE

APRIL 30, 1961

Are TV westerns making
Americans gun-happy?
PAGE 6

WHERE SHOULD DAD BE
WHEN THE BABY IS BORN?
PAGE 14

JAN AND MARION DIETRICH: FIRST ASTRONAUT TWINS PAGE 8

Chapter 6

Regret to Advise . . .

September 1961

Twelve women prepared to follow in Cobb's footsteps: to go to Pensacola for the next round of tests. They juggled their jobs and shifted around their responsibilities, so they would be ready to go. The first tests had taken a week. This time they needed two.

Gene Nora Stumbough's boss said that she couldn't have the time off. So she quit.

Sarah Gorelick had the same problem. She had already taken vacation time to go to Albuquerque. When she asked for more time off, the answer was no. So *she* quit. Her coworkers threw her a party and gave her a space helmet with her name on it.

Irene Leverton's boss—who had already demoted her after the first round of testing—told her to forget it. She, too, walked away from her job to pursue her dream.

Jerri Sloan fared a bit better. Cobb wrote a letter to Sloan's boss on her behalf, playing up her position as a NASA consultant and mentioning Flickinger, as well as the fact that *Life* magazine would likely cover the story when it broke. It worked like a charm.

And, of course, once again, babysitters needed to be lined up. Fridges stocked. Travel plans made.

The excitement grew.

The main attraction was the testing. But this was also going to be the first time these women had ever come together as a group.

The cover story of the April 1961 *Parade* magazine captured the attention of young women pilots all over the country.

The women needed to complete just one more step—the round of tests Cobb had taken at Pensacola. Once hard science showed that Cobb's results were not just the results of one exceptional woman but an indication of what women in general could do, NASA would have a hard time explaining why women should not be included in the space program.

The press did not know exactly what was going on, but an April article in *Parade* magazine made them aware that Lovelace had been comparing female test results with the results of the Mercury 7. Then, two weeks before the women were due to arrive in Pensacola, *McCall's* ran an article on Marion Dietrich's phase-one testing. As the public started to get wind of what was happening, they sent letters of support. Young women who wanted to be astronauts wrote to NASA as well.

The struggle was not just between the thirteen women who hoped to soar into space and those determined to keep them on the ground. The larger questions suddenly being put forth in articles, editorials, cartoons, and letters were, "What is a woman capable of?" "What is a woman's place?"

Jane Hart reflected on that a year later and saw it clearly: "The more extreme reaction has taken the form of editorials and columns prattling about nail polish, cookie crumbs, floating bobbie pins, and lipstick. Perhaps these men have had an exclusive lifetime exposure to frivolous, fatuous, and feather-brained women? Thus they are not aware that there is another kind, and more's the pity for them."

Men were not the only ones who found the idea of women in space unsettling. The wife of Mercury 7 astronaut James Lovell later told the *New York Times,* "I don't think they ever found a woman capable of being an astronaut. I think they would have a lot of problems on a long journey if they took a woman along."

Twelve women, urged on by Cobb and Lovelace, were ready and waiting to be tested. But here was the twist: only the navy had the facilities in which to conduct the tests. The navy had informally agreed to let Cobb use their equipment. Would they agree again? As much as *McCall's* had wanted to honor the women, all the publicity about Lovelace's program suddenly made it a public-relations headache for NASA. Americans wanted to know what NASA's position on women was, and NASA wasn't ready to answer.

Suddenly—amid all the women's anticipation, all the packing and planning— disaster struck.

Just days before the women were to join Cobb in Pensacola, Jerrie's phone rang.

It was Lovelace.

Bad news.

"The navy has canceled the tests."

"What happened?"

"I don't know. I just had a call from Pensacola saying it's off. That's all I can tell you."

Cobb called everyone she could think of, trying to get someone on the phone to explain what had happened. She was transferred from one person to the next, and no one had any answers. Most people she spoke with didn't even seem to know what she was talking about. Testing? What testing?

Cobb flew to Washington, D.C. When faced with an obstacle, she always rose to the occasion. She was going to find out what was going on if it took everything she had.

August 1961

Here are the bare facts.

Domino number one:

Vice Admiral Robert B. Pirie was the deputy chief of naval air operations. Although the Lovelace program was not news to the navy or to NASA, it was news to Pirie when he found out about the pending Pensacola testing.

Domino number two:

Pirie wrote to NASA to ensure that the proper paperwork was in order and that NASA had put in an official request, called a requirement, which would indicate an interest on NASA's part that would justify the government's spending money on a project.

Domino number three:

NASA said no. It was not their program. Therefore, they had no requirement.

Domino number four:

No requirement meant no government-spending approval, which meant there would be no testing in Pensacola.

This explanation is clear, simple, straightforward—and fairly meaningless. Yes, it was true that the navy needed the requirement from NASA. And NASA had, in fact, never given its official approval of the testing of women. But that does not explain how Pirie came to know of the impending tests, nor why, given Cobb's results, NASA chose not to give the requirement. And that is where the story of the "almost astronauts" gets deeper and darker.

At the time, though, Lovelace could not worry about the explanations. He needed to deliver the bad news to the women: there would be no further testing. This is the message they all received:

> Regret to advise arrangements at Pensacola cancelled Probably will not be possible to carry out this part of the program You may return expense advance allotment to Lovelace Foundation c/o me Letter will advise of additional developments when matter cleared further
>
> W Randolph Lovelace II MD

K Cagle was shocked. "I still can't get over how suddenly everything changed. We were notified on a Saturday afternoon not to get on a Sunday morning flight."

Rhea Hurrle was disappointed but approached it in her usual pragmatic way. "I felt terrible, but I had a job to go back to and had to go on. They never really gave us an explanation. Instead they told us not to talk about it."

Gene Nora Stumbough had a real problem. "I felt pure panic—I had no job!"

And, of course, there was an even bigger problem, one that spoke to how women were seen, or more accurately, *not* seen.

The race for space was always as much about politics as it was about science. Like many Americans, President Kennedy felt that his nation must dominate spaceflight in order to demonstrate that it was the most powerful, most forward-looking nation in the world. It didn't matter that the women were qualified—or even that they offered NASA money-saving advantages. National Air and Space Museum curator Margaret Weitekamp comments on the administration's feeling at the time: "Sending a woman to do a man's job would not project the image of international strength that Kennedy desired." That does not mean that Kennedy personally did anything to stop the tests. But it is a hint of the mood in Washington at the time. Most politicians wanted a triumph in space, with seven rugged astronaut heroes leading the way. The last thing those in power wanted was a debate over who those astronauts should be. The women were a problem, and having NASA say no to the navy was a neat, clean, efficient solution.

By canceling the Pensacola phase of testing before it began, NASA and the navy stopped the discussion. There was no need to consider sending women into space, since they had not been properly tested. Case closed. Americans who wrote private letters to NASA asking what the official word was regarding women in the space program were answered with the reply that there simply was no program for women at the current time.

NASA and the navy had sidestepped the problem for the time being.

But Lovelace was faced with a difficult dilemma. However much he thought that women could sit in the pilot's seat of space capsules, his career—and the future of the Lovelace Foundation—depended on his ability to continue working with NASA. There were other important projects in the works as well. If NASA was determined to exclude women, he needed to play along.

Mount Holyoke alumnae spoke out in favor of NASA admitting women to the space program.

Lovelace decided to back off. He sent a long letter to James Webb, assuring him that no promises had been made to the women on NASA's behalf. But Lovelace also added that he hoped the testing results to date would not go to waste and offered them to the government free of charge. After all, he was a scientist first and foremost and held on to the hope that it would be science—rather than bureaucracy or politics—that would triumph in the end.

Cobb, on the other hand, hoped that science—and fairness—would triumph sooner rather than later, and she was determined to do all she could to make that happen.

Her faith in the strength of her cause was what kept her going, kept her fighting.

And a fight was exactly what was coming.

The first challenge had been a rather straightforward one: proving that women were *capable* of being astronauts. That was a scientific matter.

Now women needed to prove that they had the *right* to be astronauts. That was a political matter. A social one.

Cobb wrote to the others, alerting them to the fact that she might soon need them "to make a small roar."

It was time to do battle.

Lots of room in space for women

By E. K. Hopper

A MESSAGE TO YOU FROM THE PRESIDENT

In our many endeavors for a lasting peace, America's space program has a new and critical importance. The skills and imagination of our young men and women are not only welcome but urgently sought in this vital area. I know they will meet this challenge to them and to the nation with vigor and resourcefulness.

John F. Kennedy

John F. Kennedy

Chapter 7

Let's Stop This Now!

Jerrie Cobb vs. NASA

The fight was completely uneven. On one side was Jerrie Cobb. On the other was NASA, which made all of the decisions about how America was going to explore space. NASA's stonewalling was backed by the expressed or implied attitudes of many politicians in Washington. What could Jerrie do? Speak up, speak out, try to influence public opinion.

Cobb flew around the country, speaking on behalf of women and how they could benefit the space program. She was, after all, a NASA consultant. In November, she went to a NASA meeting in Nassau, the Bahamas, to continue to plead her case. In a postcard sent to K Cagle from that meeting, she wrote, "Still nothing new to report. I keep trying but decisions keep getting put off till after the 1st of the year."

Then she got word from Hiden T. Cox. He worked for NASA's department of public affairs—which meant that Cobb's plight had been relegated to a public-relations issue. This could not be good news.

It wasn't. He wrote, "The future use of women astronauts is possible, but at what time in the future programs is another matter entirely. Despite the manifest interest in your proposal from audiences who hear you speak, I am afraid that at the present we cannot undertake an additional program training women to be astronauts." NASA was treating Cobb like an annoying child who did not quite know her place.

At the same time that Cobb and the other women were fighting for their right to participate in the space program, this message from President John F. Kennedy encouraging girls to get involved, appeared in the December 1961 issue of the Girl Scouts magazine, *American Girl*.

Webb took the next step. In December 1961, he wrote to Cobb, his chosen "consultant": "Under the circumstances, and since we have not found a productive relationship that could fit you into our program, I am wondering if there is any advantage to continue the consulting relationship that you and I had in mind." This was more of a suggestion than a directive. Cobb was smart enough to realize that until NASA officially ended the relationship, she was still their consultant, even though the organization never contacted her. But when her contract came up for renewal, it simply expired.

Cobb continued to speak out anyway. Perhaps her hope was kept alive by a public position President Kennedy took that was the complete opposite of the focus on male strength that Margaret Weitekamp had identified behind the scenes. Kennedy sent out public appeals such as "A Message to You from the President" asking girls to consider the space program because "the skills and imagination of our young men and women are not only welcome but urgently sought in this vital area." Kennedy seemed to stand for youth, progress, a vibrant America. An America not afraid to change. Cobb could relate.

February 1962

The NASA-sponsored First Women's Space Symposium was held at the Ambassador Hotel in Los Angeles. Cobb was introduced as the nation's first woman astronaut and spread the word to the large crowd about her testing results, as well as the results of the others. "The race for space will not be a short one—nor an easy one—but it is one in which we must all participate. Let us go forward, then—there *is* space for women!"

Cobb was excellent at speaking to the public, but the battle needed to be carried to Washington, where decisions were made. That was a perfect job for Jane Hart.

Hart was furious when the Pensacola testing was canceled. She was no shrinking violet. She had been raised to fight for what she believed in. And she firmly believed that this had become a political issue—an infringement of women's rights. Why shouldn't girls play team sports, rent cars, borrow money from a bank to buy a home or open a business . . . be astronauts? Hart was well aware that women were still fighting their way into the field of aviation. She wrote, "Just as in the past fifty years women have striven for equal opportunities to make their contribution in the air age, so, too, will they struggle and eventually succeed in the space age."

Alan Shepard and Deke Slayton—two of the Mercury 7—later admitted their opinion of the idea of female astronauts in their book *Moon Shot: The Inside Story of America's Race to the Moon*. They wrote about the qualities an astronaut should possess and added, "and, of course, no women, thank you."

Hart and Cobb knew that they were dealing with an attitude of "Who do these women think they are?" Space gals. Astronettes. Astrodolls. That's what the newspapers called them. The world already knew that the Mercury 7 had the Right Stuff. And there were plenty more men where they came from, ready and willing to follow in their footsteps. What did they need women for? What could women do except slow things down, muddle things up, get in the way?

But Hart was undaunted. The wife of Senator Philip Hart of Michigan, she had the advantage of knowing the ropes in Washington, the political ins and outs.

First, she wrote letters to all the members of the Senate and House space committees. She brought up the fact that one of the requirements for becoming an astronaut was that you had to have been a jet test pilot, but only men in the military were allowed to be jet test pilots. She knew that large organizations can discriminate simply by following existing rules. Hart also knew that rules such as this can be challenged when officials are under the spotlight of public questioning.

Mercury 7 astronauts Alan Shepard and Donald "Deke" Slayton

Hart was tireless, lobbying to resume the women's testing. She found the right ally in Liz Carpenter, Vice President Lyndon B. Johnson's executive assistant. (Carpenter was the first woman executive assistant to a vice president.) Johnson was not only the vice president; he was also the head of the National Aeronautics and Space Council. Through Carpenter, Hart and Cobb could reach the one man who had the power to lean on NASA.

Hart ran through the main points of the story for Carpenter, telling her about how well they had done on the tests and that the Pensacola tests had suddenly been canceled because the navy did not receive the required paperwork from NASA. Carpenter was sympathetic and agreed to bring it to Johnson's attention and to see if the vice president would meet with Cobb and Hart to discuss the situation.

The Vice President Weighs In

The women had one big chance to make their case.

To brief Johnson for the meeting, Carpenter wrote him a memo. She summarized what she had learned from Cobb and Hart and gave Johnson her opinion: "I think you could get a good press out of this if you can tell Mrs. Hart and Miss Cobb something affirmative. The story about women astronauts is getting a big play and I hate for them to come here and not go away with some encouragement." Carpenter then drafted a letter for Johnson to send to James Webb and noted in her memo, "Do you think you could write the attached letter to Dr. Webb, and show it to them [Hart and Cobb] before they leave."

The letter Carpenter drafted for Johnson to Webb included the statement in the very first paragraph "I'm sure you agree that sex should not be a reason for disqualifying a candidate for orbital flight."

Carpenter was thorough. She set everything up for Johnson. All he had to do was sign the letter and say the right words.

He did not—and therein lies one of the most troubling, and revealing, strands in this whole story, one that did not come to light until decades later.

Johnson took Carpenter's letter and wrote *Let's Stop This Now!* in large letters across the bottom, followed by the word *File.*

And filed it was. The letter was never sent on to Webb. It stayed with Johnson's papers for nearly forty years, when it was discovered by Margaret Weitekamp while she was researching her book *Right Stuff, Wrong Sex: America's First Women in Space Program.*

Johnson was angry and determined to end any possibility that Cobb, Hart, and the other women would go into space. But why? Why did he care so much? In fact, when he later became president, Johnson—the same man who wrote *Let's Stop This Now!* on that fateful letter—signed an affirmative-action plan to make federal agencies *actively* give women and minorities equal employment opportunities. Jerrie Cobb knew Johnson's reasons but did not reveal them until 2007. She spoke with me that May.

Cobb and I were sitting in a hotel lobby in Oshkosh, Wisconsin. Also present were Gene Nora Stumbough Jessen, Jerri Sloan Truhill, K Cagle, B Steadman, Irene Leverton, Sarah Gorelick Ratley, and Rhea Hurrle Woltman. The women had just been honored by the University of

Wisconsin at Oshkosh for their achievements. I was hoping to learn what was said in that office when Cobb and Hart met with Johnson. Knowing how reserved and polite Cobb is, I never expected what came next.

She took a breath and shook her head a little. Then she told me that Johnson had looked at her and said, "Jerrie, if we let you or other women into the space program, we'd have to let blacks in. We'd have to let Mexican Americans in, and Chinese Americans. We'd have to let every minority in, and we just can't do it."

My eyes opened wide. I couldn't believe my ears. Until that day in May, the only damning evidence against Johnson was the *Let's Stop This Now!* letter. I was stunned. The man who was vice president, who would soon become president, had described in one startling line the blind prejudice the women were up against. It was prejudice—against women, African Americans, Hispanics, Asians—that had kept the women on the ground.

"Can I use that?" I asked her. She wasn't sure. She is by nature un-comfortable saying anything negative about anyone. In a thank-you note she sent to Johnson after the meeting, she had referred to his comment by saying simply, "You mentioned minority groups which wanted repre-sentation as astronauts," and went on to make the point that women were not actually a minority group.

And then, in the Wisconsin hotel lobby the evening news came on. We watched as the cameras cut to an interview with Cobb. And then I heard it—for the second time: Johnson's comment about having to let minorities into the space program if he let in the women. Cobb slapped me on the leg in surprise—she hadn't remembered she had said that out loud to the reporter. "Well, there you have it—I said it on the air, so go ahead and use it!" I told her I would.

So there it was: the hard wall of prejudice that lay behind NASA's bland rules about jet pilots. In fact, just as Cobb and Hart were meeting with Johnson, the civil rights movement was gathering momentum in the South. That inspired the highly es-teemed and popular TV broadcaster Edward R. Murrow to ask NASA administrator James Webb: "Why don't we put the first nonwhite man in space?" That would cer-tainly send a message that might improve race relations.

SCIENCE
Space

THE VICE PRESIDENT
WASHINGTON
March 15, 1962

Dear Jim:

I have conferred with Mrs. Philip Hart and Miss Jerrie Cobb concerning their effort to get women utilized as astronauts. I'm sure you agree that sex should not be a reason for disqualifying a candidate for orbital flight.

Could you advise me whether NASA has disqualified anyone because of being a woman?

As I understand it, two principal requirements for orbital flight at this stage are: 1) that the individual be experienced at high speed military test flying; and 2) that the individual have an engineering background enabling him to take over controls in the event it became necessary.

Would you advise me whether there are any women who meet these qualifications?

If not, could you estimate for me the time when orbital flight will have become sufficiently safe that these two requirements are no longer necessary and a larger number of individuals may qualify?

I know we both are grateful for the desire to serve on the part of these women, and look forward to the time when they can.

Sincerely,

Lets stop this now!

Lyndon B. Johnson

File

Mr. James E. Webb
Administrator
National Aeronautics and Space Administration
Washington, D. C.

TRANSFERRED TO HANDWRITING FILE

COPY LBJ LIBRARY

This is the letter on which Vice President Lyndon B. Johnson scrawled his opinion on women in the space program. Instead of sending the letter, which had been drafted for him by his assistant Liz Carpenter, Johnson relegated it to his files, where it remained hidden for nearly forty years.

Cobb and Hart were actually doing more than battling against the attitude that women belonged at home—they were also challenging the view that America's heroes must be white. Now that Johnson's scrawled message—and Cobb's recollection—have been made public, we can all see that. But at the time, the governmental organizations were very careful not to show their hands. They claimed they were just following the rules. As Weitekamp notes in her book, "Both organizations [NASA and the navy] had taken care not to commit their opposition to paper. . . . Officials at both agencies recognized that they could not be seen as dismissing women's concerns outright."

If Johnson had taken Carpenter's advice, the women might well have joined the space program. Instead, he revealed the huge obstacle they were facing. But even that did not stop them. Just a few days after their meeting with Johnson, Hart spoke to a group of five hundred women. A woman in that audience then wrote a letter to Johnson that said, in part, "We would like to urge you to continue in every way possible with this test program for we believe women have a part to play in this vital aspect of our century. . . . We want to do something more important than drink tea, play bridge, and sit on the side lines while there are vital things we can do."

Johnson replied, "I welcome your letter which has come along with a great many others about women astronauts. . . . One must be a graduate of a test-pilot school. . . . When women who meet all the requirements apply, and in time I expect some will, then they will get equal opportunities with men."

There it was—again. The built-in roadblock. Being a jet test pilot.

There could never be "women who meet all the requirements" until women were allowed to be jet test pilots.

Other women wrote to Johnson, too. The reply was the same.

Yet in Washington, no one official—even if it is the vice president—ever gets the final word. The women's cause was attracting the interest of members of Congress.

Representative George Miller, of the House Committee on Science and Astronautics, thought the story was worth investigating. He contacted his committee chairman, Congressman Victor Anfuso. Cobb flew to Washington to meet with Anfuso. And in June, a special subcommittee hearing on the topic of astronaut qualifications was announced. It would be held in July.

This was not a meeting in a private office. Finally, Cobb and Hart could speak out, and NASA would have to defend itself in public. Perhaps the battle was not so unequal after all.

Chapter 8

Jerrie Cobb Isn't Running This Program. I Am!

July 17, 1962: Ten a.m., the Hearing

Cobb and Hart sat at the witness table. The room was full. Spectators were crowded into their section. The press was there in full force. In front of Cobb and Hart sat eleven U.S. representatives ready to hear their testimony. Two of them were women.

Chairman Victor Anfuso began the hearings by stating their purpose. They were there to evaluate the qualifications for selecting astronauts and to ensure that those qualifications "should not be prejudged or prequalified by the fact that these talents happen to be possessed by men or women." He then invited Cobb to speak.

Cobb steeled her nerves. She had practiced her speech, had made notes in the margin about where to pause, where to smile. She was ready.

Cobb said, "We seek, only, a place in our nation's space future without discrimination. We ask as citizens of this nation to be allowed to participate with seriousness and sincerity in the making of history now, as women have in the past."

Today this seems so right, so obvious, that it may be hard to understand how anyone could disagree. But in 1962 it was not at all clear that women had the right to be our heroes alongside men. Cobb reported on the testing that she and the other women had completed. She also gave brief profiles of the eleven other women, not present, making the identities of all members of the group known to the public for the first time.

Jerrie Cobb and Jane Hart during their testimony at the congressional hearings in July 1962

The reporters at the press tables scribbled furiously. In different parts of the country these women's phone lines soon began to ring.

Knowing that the government is always sensitive about financial concerns, Cobb addressed that as well, telling the subcommittee both that no taxpayer dollars had been spent on the women thus far and that if women were utilized, it would save NASA a significant amount of money. And she informed them of the scientific data that showed that "women are less susceptible to monotony, loneliness, heat, cold, pain and noise than the opposite sex." Cobb also made it clear that this was not "a battle of the sexes" and that women simply wanted "to be part of the research and participation in space exploration."

Near the end of her statement, she also pointed out that "no nation has yet sent a human female into space." This fact was well known by those in power. Russia had plans in the works to send a woman into space. It was only a matter of time before they succeeded. Cobb assumed that one of America's priorities would be to get there first.

No Laughing Matter

What came next was extremely unfortunate: a bad joke at the absolutely wrong time, made by the wrong person, the chairman of the subcommittee, Victor Anfuso. After thanking Cobb for her statement, he said, "I think that we can safely say at this time that the whole purpose of space exploration is to someday colonize these other planets, and I don't see how we can do that without women."

Laughter followed.

Hart was next. As a mother of eight children, with a strong sense of will and wit, she jabbed back: "I would like to say, I couldn't help but notice that you call upon me immediately after you referred to colonizing space."

Hart then thanked the subcommittee for the opportunity—and went right to it. She saw what was at issue—that it was not just the rules being examined but the attitudes behind them as well. "It is inconceivable to me that the world of outer space should be restricted to men only, like some sort of stag club. . . . Now, no woman can get up and seriously discuss a subject like this without being painfully aware that her talk is going to inspire a lot of condescending little smiles and mildly humorous winks. But, happily for the nation, there have always been men, men like the members of this committee, who have helped women succeed in roles that they were previously thought incapable of handling."

Hart pointed out that during the Civil War many believed that women could never be hospital attendants or go into the field to take care of the sick and dying. But women fought for that right and won, going on to save countless lives. Hart said, "A woman in space today is no more preposterous than a woman in a field hospital one hundred years ago."

Hart knew her American history and understood that whether or not women were given opportunities often depended on what men were doing. As we've seen, it was when men went off to war that women were given the good jobs in the factories. Hart did not think this pattern made sense. "It seems to me," Hart said, "a basic error in American thought that the only time women are allowed to make a full contribution to a better nation is when there is a manpower shortage."

Hart was eloquent. She talked about the need for women to have equal choices when it came to education and said that if girls grow up to be homemakers, there is nothing wrong with that—as long as it is their choice and not something they settle into for lack of other options. "Let's face it," she said. "For many women the PTA just is not enough."

When Hart was finished, the lights were dimmed and Cobb showed some pictures of the testing. Once the subcommittee had an understanding of what testing had been completed and what had been canceled, discussion resumed.

Talk turned quickly to the jet-test-pilot issue. This was the sticking point. The committee wanted to be sure they grasped the situation fully. Although the WASP had been able to fly military aircraft during the war, women were banned from doing so after the end of the WASP in 1944. Yet one piece of news came as a surprise to the subcommittee—that other countries, including Russia, already allowed women to be jet test pilots. Cobb also repeatedly made the point that she was not asking for NASA to eliminate the criterion, just to acknowledge that the women had "an equivalent experience in flying."

So far, Cobb and Hart had been well spoken, in command of their facts. You might think they were winning. But everything was about to change. For there was an actor in this whole drama who had not yet come on stage. This was her moment.

During the questioning, a woman had entered the room. Blond, well dressed, and polished. Her entrance was hard to miss.

Hart and Cobb had been heard. It was now time for this third witness to speak.

Jerrie Cobb Isn't Running This Program. I Am!

69

Anfuso introduced her with unabashed admiration.

"I have the honor and privilege of welcoming Miss Jacqueline Cochran, who, without a question, is the foremost woman pilot in the world and who holds more national and international speed, distance, and altitude records than any other living person."

Cochran had the floor. After describing her own accomplishments and awards in detail, she got to the point: "I do not believe there has been any intentional or actual discrimination against women in the astronaut program to date."

Strike one!

Here, she digressed from her prepared statement into a lengthy description of all the things jet test pilots do that are important. Despite her comment that she was speaking "more or less off the cuff," Cochran had carefully prepared and distributed her statement to many people the month before the hearing. Copies were sent to Vice President Johnson, James Webb, Robert Pirie, and other officials. She also sent it to Lovelace, Jane Hart, and Gene Nora Stumbough.

With her digression behind her, Cochran continued with her statement.

"There is no shortage of well-trained and long-experienced male pilots to serve as astronauts. . . ."

Strike two!

"No woman should be selected as an astronaut trainee unless a sufficient group of women are simultaneously selected so that norms can be established rather than merely the individual capabilities of one or a few who might not be representative of women as a whole."

Strike three!

If Lyndon Johnson and the prejudiced attitudes he spoke for were one wall blocking the women, Cochran stood as another. But why? Why would a woman—arguably America's greatest woman pilot, for that matter—walk in and give such damaging testimony? Did she not want them to succeed? And if not, why?

How Jackie Saw It

Jackie Cochran played a complicated role in this story from early on. From the first, Lovelace needed funds to pay for his Woman in Space program. A lot of that funding came from Jackie Cochran and her husband, Floyd Odlum, who was chairman of

Jackie Cochran was the first woman to break the sound barrier. Standing by her plane is friend and famed pilot Chuck Yeager, who was the first person to break the sound barrier.

the Lovelace Foundation's board of trustees. She and her husband were also close personal friends of Lovelace, and he was her personal physician.

Cochran got involved with the program in November 1960. She assumed that Lovelace was bringing her on in a leadership role and immediately wrote him a long letter detailing suggestions for how the program should be run. Not surprisingly, one of Cochran's recommendations was to change the age requirements for testing, which would have allowed her to be eligible.

Jerrie Cobb Isn't Running This Program. I Am!

71

Lovelace quietly ignored her directives. It's likely that he didn't want to get into a conflict with his friend.

Cochran then tried a different tactic. She simply assumed that she would be one of the women tested and approached the issue as a matter of scheduling, sending Lovelace memos about when she was available for which tests: "I'll take that bicycle test Monday." And, "I can take some of the tests you have in mind on Monday or possibly on Tuesday morning." But none of Cochran's maneuvering got her what she wanted.

Furious, she threatened to pull her funding. Sarah Gorelick happened to be at the clinic doing her testing that week and heard Cochran letting loose, screaming and yelling at Lovelace. He held his ground and told her the truth—that her age and previous health conditions prevented her from being a candidate.

The friction continued.

Arriving at the Lovelace Clinic one day to discover candidates being tested who were not on her suggested list further provoked her. She couldn't stomach being out of the loop. She was especially irritated by the special attention that Jerrie Cobb seemed to be enjoying from Lovelace.

Cochran also resented the media's interest in Cobb. After Cobb was featured in *Life* and *Time* magazines, Cochran put together a piece for *Parade* magazine about two of the women whom she had handpicked: the twins, Jan and Marion Dietrich. The headline read, WOMEN IN SPACE: FAMED AVIATRIX PREDICTS WOMEN ASTRONAUTS WITHIN SIX YEARS. The byline: Jacqueline Cochran. She was the famed aviatrix, of course. The front-page photo showed Jan Dietrich on a treadmill. The authoritative figure in the back, clipboard in hand, was Cochran. And for those paying attention, there was no mistaking the jab at Jerrie Cobb in Cochran's call for more candidates in her closing line: "You might become the first woman astronaut who really earns that name."

Cochran hated that Cobb was viewed by the public as the leader of the group. She didn't want the twelve other women looking at Cobb that way, either. She sent each of the women—except for Jerrie—a letter in July 1961, detailing her leadership role in the program, explaining that she was footing the bill for transportation and meals because she believed that "a properly organized astronaut program for women would be a fine thing." She went on to encourage them to be in the best physical shape possible, not to smoke, and not to talk to the press until they came together as a group at the end of their testing.

Cochran's feelings about Cobb shone through on more than one occasion. After the women were first told about the Pensacola opportunity, Cochran asked Jerri Sloan if she was prepared to go. Sloan responded, "Yes, I certainly am, but Jerrie hasn't told us when." Cochran shot back, "Jerrie! Jerrie has nothing to do with this. I'm heading this up!" When Sloan mentioned that Cobb was the one who had told her she had passed her phase-one tests, Cochran exploded: "Jerrie Cobb isn't running this program. I am!"

It especially ticked Cochran off that James Webb had made Cobb a special consultant at NASA. After all, it was Cochran who was president of the Fédération Aéronautique Internationale (FAI) at the time, not Cobb. It was Cochran who could have been enjoying the spotlight. She hated not being in the know when reporters questioned her about Lovelace's program. They assumed she would be in on all the details, and Cochran became more and more annoyed with Lovelace—and with Cobb.

And as to the question of how Vice Admiral Pirie had found out about the Lovelace program—information that set into motion a chain of events that directly resulted in the navy's canceling the Pensacola testing—well, he found out from Cochran. She hadn't disclosed anything that was a secret; nevertheless, the day she got in Pirie's car was the beginning of the end for the Lovelace women.

That seemingly simple sequence of events had behind it men like Alan Shepard and Deke Slayton, who did not want women in space; politicians like Johnson, who were dead set against opening a door that would let nonmale, nonwhite Americans into space; and one wealthy, influential, and extremely determined woman whose pride had been injured.

All this history came to a head when Cochran walked into that courtroom. She was decidedly *not* in Cobb and Hart's corner.

Cochran Turns the Tables

Cochran's testimony continued with a full-blown proposal for a different project, one she had alluded to in that July 1961 letter to the twelve women: a slow, organized study of a large group of women over a long period of time. Her reason for wanting to study a large group? She expected volunteers to drop out "due to marriage, childbirth, and other causes." Cochran then offered to lead this proposed project.

Jackie Cochran was a complicated person. Although she spoke out against Jerrie Cobb and helped to hold the "Mercury 13" women back, she also led the Women's Airforce Service Pilots (WASP) with honor.

Anfuso pressed for clarification on Cochran's position.

"Miss Cochran, you do believe that women belong in the space program?"

Cochran: "I certainly think the research should be done. Then I can tell you afterward."

With that, Cochran effectively turned the entire thrust of the conversation away from the issue on the table, which Hart and Cobb represented, toward a discussion of a completely different project for women—a new project, to be run by Cochran.

Cochran was the person who had organized the WASP during World War II. At that time, she was a trailblazer who championed women. She was an American heroine in her own right. But she was also a woman who had made her way in life on her own astonishing willpower. She came from nothing, growing up dirt-poor and dressed in rags; her family moved from mill town to mill town, scraping to get by. She fought for everything she got in life. As she grew older, the girl born Bessie Pittman reinvented herself. She claimed not to be part of her biological family and left her true identity behind. When Bessie Pittman moved to New York City in 1929, she became Jacqueline Cochran and never looked back. Jackie Cochran was a person who would do just about anything to make the world fit her sense of what it should be. And she did not think women should go into space unless *she* figured prominently in the plan.

Does Jackie Cochran's attitude reflect something about women in general that made this issue so personal, so emotional? No. In fact, if anyone was blinded by prejudice, it was members of that thoroughly male organization, NASA. The easiest way to see that is through the testimony given on the second day of hearings.

Chapter 9

The Men Go Off and Fight the Wars and Fly the Airplanes

July 18, 1962. Ten a.m.

Representative Anfuso opened by introducing the day's honored guests: "Today we have with us two Americans of heroic stature, of whom nothing further need be said." He was speaking of the Mercury 7 astronauts John Glenn and Scott Carpenter. These were the big guns. America's heroes. This was NASA's day to make its case—and it used its stars to dazzle the subcommittee.

George Low, the director of spacecraft and flight missions for NASA, began by spelling out the qualifications for being an astronaut. He implied that allowing the women to continue being tested would interfere with the needs of the program because there was not enough test equipment to go around. If women were tested, they would hold up deserving men.

But there was someone sitting in the room who knew better, even though she didn't get the chance to say so. Cathryn Walters, the graduate assistant who had put Cobb, Funk, and Hurrle through isolation testing for phase two, had come with Cobb to lend her support. She had been to the Pensacola facilities and talked with the doctors there, who were quite willing to schedule women for testing to see what their results would be. Vice Admiral Pirie had said much the same in a private letter.

Mercury 7 astronauts Scott Carpenter (left) and John Glenn (right) pose in front of a space capsule. They both testified against the women at the Congressional hearing.

John Glenn is the guest of honor in a hero's parade in Cocoa Beach, Florida, after his first orbital spaceflight. On either side of Glenn sit President John F. Kennedy (left) and General Leighton I. Davis (right).

When Scott Carpenter spoke, he dismissed the idea that the women's flying experience was anything like piloting a jet. "A person can't enter a backstroke swimming race and, by swimming twice the distance in a crawl, qualify as a backstroker."

John Glenn chimed in with a line that was either planned as an off-color joke or just sounded that way. It played perfectly on the idea that men and women up in space together would not be able to keep their minds on their work. "If we can find any women that demonstrate that they have better qualifications for going into a program than we have going into that program, we would welcome them with open arms."

Laughter rippled through the room.

Glenn quickly tried to backpedal, adding, "For the purposes of my going home this afternoon, I think that should be stricken from the record."

Glenn went on to say that he thought the media had made too much of the testing the women had gone through and that it didn't mean they were qualified for anything. "A real crude analogy," he went on, "might be: We have the Washington

Redskins football team. My mother could probably pass the physical exam that they give preseason for the Redskins, but I doubt if she could play too many games for them."

With their jokes about swimming and football, Carpenter and Glenn sounded like regular guys, plainspoken men—the kind of heroes that made America proud.

The Pilot Paradox

And then it came back to the test-pilot issue again: When President Eisenhower created NASA, back in 1958, there was much discussion over what qualifications potential astronauts would need. Some suggested that they should come from fields that demanded bravery, such as exploration and mountain climbing. Then someone suggested that pilots might make the most sense; after all, they were talking about putting some kind of craft into space, and pilots were trained to fly. Test pilots had the added advantage of being trained to learn how to fly newly designed craft that had never been flown before.

No doubt, the qualifications made sense. But at the time, jet test pilots were, by definition, military men. Women were simply not allowed in. So once it was decided that potential astronaut candidates must be jet test pilots, women were excluded. The problem was not that being a jet test pilot didn't make sense as a qualification for an astronaut; it was that under the current rules, women had *no chance of becoming* jet test pilots.

And yet NASA had already bent its own rules. According to regulations, astronauts needed to have college degrees. John Glenn didn't, but the requirement was waived for him. NASA could have found a way to evaluate woman fliers who had not had the chance to be jet test pilots; it chose not to.

One of the representatives on the subcommittee, a woman, said that the jet-pilot rule was "a definite roadblock against" women. And it was right then, at that moment, that John Glenn put into words the real issue behind the end to the women's testing, behind the vice president's resistance, behind the jokes directed at the women.

Glenn said, "I think this gets back to the way our social order is organized, really. It is just a fact. The men go off and fight the wars and fly the airplanes and come back and help design and build and test them. The fact that women are not in this field is a fact of our social order."

Cartoon by Jim Lange from the July 19, 1962, edition of the *Daily Oklahoman*

Cobb and Hart and the other women—just like the civil rights protesters in the South—knew that the social order needed to change. Glenn, Carpenter, Low, Johnson, and others used rules, regulations, prejudices revealed only behind closed doors, to resist—to keep things as they were. With the collaboration of an angry woman, the voices of the status quo got their way, and the social order stood.

This was clear when one subcommittee member said, "If today our priority program is getting a man on the moon, maybe we should ask the good ladies to be patient and let us get this thing accomplished first and then go after training woman astronauts."

Despite little jokes that cropped up during these hearings—about women being handy at diffusing tension or making good company on long trips—not one person ever argued that the women were not strong enough or smart enough or capable enough to be astronauts.

And then the hearings were adjourned. Just like that. No mention of the third day of hearings that were supposed to follow on the next day. Just a thank-you from Anfuso to Glenn and Carpenter for their testimony as he pointed out how many mothers had come to the hearings with their children in order to catch sight of the famous astronauts.

The room was emptying.

It was over.

Outer Space Restricted to Men

Cobb and Hart couldn't believe it. What about the third day—their chance for a rebuttal? Cobb did not give up. She submitted her comments anyway, to be included in the hearing records. "We ask to complete the tests originally scheduled and that the successful candidates go on to even more rigorous tests and astronaut training. All

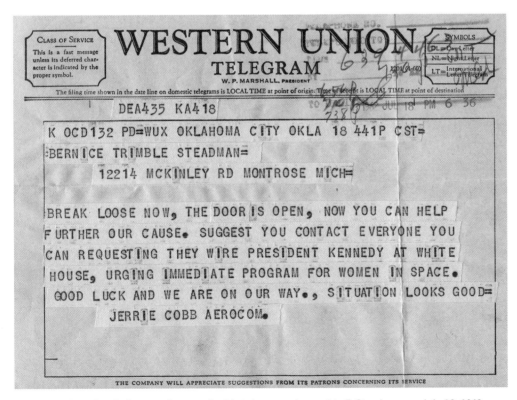

Cobb's continued optimism can be seen in this telegram she sent to B Steadman on July 18, 1962.

we need is the opportunity to prove that we are 'capable,' 'qualified,' and 'required.'"

But Cochran was determined not to let Cobb have the last word.

She turned in her own notes for the record. "First: There is not now and to date has not been any women-in-space or woman-astronaut program. Second: No woman to date has passed Mercury astronaut tests. I have the word of Dr. Lovelace on that. The tests . . . did not qualify any person as an astronaut or astronaut candidate." She went on to scold, "Women for one reason or another have always come into each phase of aviation a little behind their brothers. They should, I believe, accept this delay and not get into the hair of the public authorities about it."

Aviation historian Deborah Douglas later summed up the situation: "It didn't matter that Jane Hart had the clout to get a hearing. Jackie Cochran had the clout to end the ambitions of the women in this program."

Jane Hart did not add anything to her statement. Very likely she saw the writing on the wall during the hearings. Afterward she wrote, "In the recent congressional hearings, a NASA representative was asked if the integration of the thirteen women astronaut candidates would stop the manned flight to the moon project. He replied with an unqualified 'yes'! [The exact quote from George Low was "Very much so."] If thirteen women can bring a forty-billion-dollar program to a grinding halt, it is a mighty sick program. For the sake of our nation, let us hope the answer was just childish."

In the end, the report put out by the subcommittee did not recommend any change to NASA's qualifications for astronauts nor that the Pensacola testing for the women be resumed. It did recommend that a testing program for women exist at some point but deferred to NASA on all details. James Webb appointed Cochran to be Cobb's replacement as NASA's special consultant. But her consultant status had no effect — it changed nothing about opportunities for women at NASA.

Jane Hart made her feelings known in a magazine article she published later that year, restating part of her testimony that "It is inconceivable that the vast world of outer space should be restricted to men."

Truhill spoke out, too. "The guys didn't want us at NASA—that's clear. The remarks they made about us were so degrading and ungentlemanlike. One NASA official said he'd rather send up monkeys than a bunch of women."

And once again, the press weighed in. Editorial cartoons showed a female astronaut decorating a space capsule; another portrayed an "astronette" applying lipstick while flying. But some cartoons agreed with the women's point of view.

NASA Administrator James Webb swears Jackie Cochran in as a NASA consultant on June 11, 1963.

Fellow Oklahoman Jim Lange showed his support of Jerrie Cobb with this editorial cartoon published in the July 27, 1962 *Daily Oklahoman*.

Dr. Donald Kilgore, who conducted some of the tests on the women at the Lovelace Clinic, later remarked on their work ethic. "The other thing that was striking about the women was that they were more pliable than the men. They didn't gripe as much. When they were told they had to be in bed at seven o'clock, they went to bed at seven o'clock. When they were told they had to take an enema before going to bed and take an enema when they woke up, they did it. They didn't protest. And they didn't give any reasons why they shouldn't do it. So they didn't complain as much."

Only one scientific paper on the Lovelace tests done in New Mexico was ever published. A 1964 issue of the *American Journal of Obstetrics and Gynecology* discussed the testing and theorized that menstrual cycles did, in fact, interfere with women's abilities to work in space! However, Cathryn Walters took the data from the tank testing she and Shurley had conducted and used it in a larger study, which demonstrated that women handle the stress of isolation better than men do.

Lovelace was made the new director of space medicine at NASA in 1964. Tragically, he and his wife were killed in a plane crash a year later.

Right Stuff, Wrong Time

The summer after the hearings, on June 16, 1963, Valentina Tereshkova became the first woman to fly in space. The Russians had gotten there first. But Tereshkova was neither a pilot nor a scientist. She was simply a passenger. Cobb later met Tereshkova: "She told me I was her role model," Cobb said. "The first thing she said to me was, 'We always figured you would be first. What happened?'"

Since NASA had kept women out of space, it likely did not feel the need to explain "what happened." Instead, it announced that there were many women working at the agency in other capacities. But the underlying attitude toward women came shining through in a speech that NASA's astronaut-training officer Robert Voas gave that year. He said, "I think we all look forward to the time when women will be a part of our spaceflight team, for when this time arrives, it will mean that men will really have found a home in space—for the woman is the personification of the home." In other words, a woman's place was still in the kitchen!

The thirteen women who were almost astronauts had the Right Stuff. The problem was that they were the wrong sex and it was the wrong time. They were not able to change the "social order." Not right away, that is.

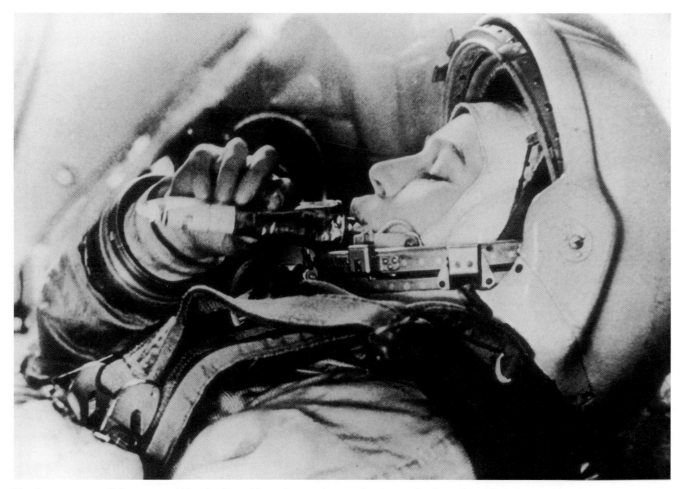

The first woman to fly into space, Valentina Tereshkova, is seen here eating from a feeding tube while in her space suit.

Rhea Seddon

Shannon Lucid

Bonnie Dunbar

Mary Cle

17

Jernigan

18

Millie Hughes-Fulford

USA

19

Roberta Bondar

Canada

20

Jan Davis

USA

28

Eileen Collins

USA

30

awrence

Catherine C

USA

37

Kavandi

ndre-Deshays

43

THE MERCURY 13

EMALE PILOTS WHO PAVED THE WAY!

Chapter 10

NASA Never Had any Intention of Putting Those Women in Space

Making Their Mark

Looking back on the events of 1962 more than thirty years later, astronaut Scott Carpenter summed up his view of what had happened: "NASA never had any intention of putting those women in space. The whole idea was foisted upon it, and it was happy to have the research data, but those women were before their time."

But that phrase, "before their time," gets right to the heart of the problem. Why should there ever be a particular time that's right or wrong for any group of people? It's not that the thirteen women were outsiders trying to push their way in where they didn't belong. It's that what John Glenn called the "social order" of the time shut out strong, qualified women not because they weren't capable enough but *because* they were women. The evidence of their capabilities lies in the many ways these thirteen women went on to make their mark on the world. They continued to fly, push the boundaries of their field, and show what women are made of.

Wally Funk has been flying for more than fifty years and has helped move the aviation field forward for women. In 1971, she became the first female inspector for the Federal Aviation Administration (FAA), and in 1974, she was appointed one of the first female air-safety investigators for the National Transportation Safety Board. Wally remains determined to be among the early U.S. tourists in space. To train for this, she has tried the Apollo static space simulator at Edwards Air Force Base and traveled to

In March 2007, Myrtle "K" Cagle (left) and Wally Funk (right) visited the International Women's Air & Space Museum in Cleveland, Ohio.

Star City, Russia, for one week of cosmonaut training, during which she experienced zero-gravity conditions at their training center. She continues to teach flying, as well as to lecture at colleges.

At the time of the canceled Pensacola testing, Jerri Sloan already owned her own company. So she put her focus back on the business and kept right on flying. But not just any flying—oh, no! Some of her missions were very hush-hush. She and her new business partner, Joe Truhill—whom she later married—used their planes to ferry top-secret infrared cameras for the government. She also served on the board of directors for the International Women's Air and Space Museum. She continues to speak out whenever she witnesses discrimination against women in space and aviation.

Jean Hixson, who had been a WASP in World War II and in 1957 became the fourth woman to break the sound barrier, earning her the nickname "Supersonic Schoolmarm," went back to teaching fifth-grade math. While teaching, she continued with her aviation work, conducting space-navigation research at the Aerospace Medical Research Laboratory, at Wright-Patterson Air Force Base. She retired from the air force reserves as a full colonel in 1982, and from teaching in 1983. She died the following year.

Jerri Sloan Truhill (right) and pilot-pal Martha Ann Reading (left) get their plane ready for takeoff. Reading was the first woman lieutenant colonel in the Civil Air Patrol.

In 1978, Jean Hixson was promoted to full colonel in the air force.

Irene Leverton has been flying for more than sixty years. In 1969, she founded the Women's Airline Transport Pilots Association. She also set up the Women's Pylon Racing Association. Leverton was a pilot examiner for the FAA for fourteen years. She has been a crop-duster pilot and a corporate pilot, has taught flying, flown Civil Air Patrol searches, run an air-taxi service, and flown for the U.S. Forest Service. Irene says, "I had to give up many things over the years to be a pilot. I was always looking for adventure."

Gene Nora Stumbough found her "dream job" piloting Beech Aircraft's new model. Just as the hearings got underway, she was heading out on a three-month, forty-eight-state tour for the new airplane. Soon after, she married Bob Jessen and they started a family, as well as their own Beech Aircraft dealership. Gene Nora still flies and races whenever she can. She wrote a book about the first all women's cross-country air race—also known as the Powder Puff Derby—and is working on her second book. Gene Nora helped found the Idaho Aviation Hall of Fame and the Ninety-Nines Museum of Women Pilots, and is a past president of the Ninety-Nines organization.

Gene Nora Stumbough Jessen
still flies whenever she can.

B Steadman is also a past president of the Ninety-Nines. She kept flying and owned an aviation business in Michigan for many years. She has won every major air race for women and written a memoir about her life as a pilot called *Tethered Mercury*. B was also the cofounder and president of the International Women's Air and Space Museum.

The Dietrich twins had always done everything together as kids, even saving money for flying lessons. As adults, they forged their own paths in aviation. Marion was a writer and covered stories about flight for *Time* magazine and the *San Francisco Chronicle*. She died in 1974. Her sister Jan was the first woman to become an officer on a charter jet. She also sued World Airways for discrimination when they wouldn't let her become a pilot for their commercial airline. Jan passed away in 2008.

Myrtle "K" Cagle continued to be a flight instructor and Civil Air Patrol pilot. She worked as a certified airplane mechanic at Robins Air Force Base until 1996 and was inducted into the Georgia Aviation Hall of Fame in 2003.

Sarah Gorelick Ratley left engineering and became an accountant in her family's business before going to work for the federal government in Kansas City. She continues to fly and has competed in six Powder Puff Derby races as well as the International Women's Air Race.

Rhea Hurrle Woltman did not pursue flying as a long-term career. She has devoted her life to being a professional parliamentarian. This is someone who is hired by organizations to sit in on their meetings and help them make sure they follow their rules. In March 2008, Rhea was inducted into the Colorado Women's Hall of Fame for her service as a parliamentarian and her participation with the "Mercury 13."

Although Jerrie Cobb was saddened and disappointed by the results of the hearings, her positive spirit stayed intact. She and Hart appeared on the *Today* show shortly after the hearings were over to state their case to the American public. And she was happy to be included in *Life* magazine's special issue "One Hundred of the Most Important Young Men and Women in the United States" that fall.

But Jerrie, a deeply spiritual person, felt she had done her "share of shaking." Cobb's overriding goal was to make a meaningful contribution with her life as an aviator. She flew off to South America and has spent decades there, delivering food, medicine, and supplies to the Indians of the Amazon rain forest. In 1981, she was nominated for a Nobel Peace Prize for her work there.

Jane Hart and B Steadman stand by an experimental aircraft at the University of Michigan in 2001 after speaking to a group of female engineering students who were aspiring astronauts.

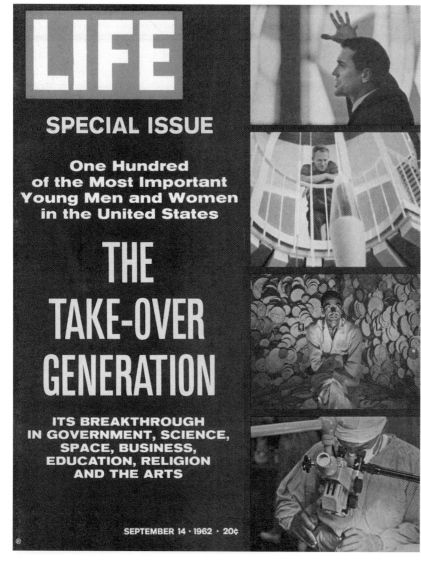

The September 14, 1962, issue of *Life* magazine featured the "Take-Over Generation." On the cover were four of the men of the "Red-Hot Hundred." Inside, a foldout, six-page section displayed photographs of the honored young men and women. The inside gallery was designed like a yearbook with a photograph of each person and a few sentences describing the accomplishments that had won him or her a spot in the issue. The list was varied and included a playwright, financier, surgeon, architect, scholars, athletes, artists, and more.

This is the photo of Jerrie Cobb that accompanied her entry. Her caption noted that she was a NASA consultant and a "likely first among the 13 U.S. women Astronaut candidates." Looking back at *Life's* selections from a twenty-first-century point of view, the list reflects the prejudices of the time. Of the 100 leaders featured in the article, 93 were white and 91 were men. This collective portrait of the new generation did not even include Dr. Martin Luther King Jr.

In 1998, Cobb got word that NASA was conducting a mission to study the aging process and was considering sending John Glenn, then seventy-seven, up again. She left the jungle, returning to Washington, D.C., to lobby for a second chance to go into space. A "Send Jerrie into Space" campaign was spearheaded and was supported by senators from California and Oklahoma, as well as the National Women's History Project, the National Organization for Women (NOW), and others. NOW circulated a petition and had Hillary Rodham Clinton's support. There was overwhelming public support in favor of giving Cobb this well-deserved chance. But only John Glenn was sent. Cobb returned to South America, where, to this day, she prefers to spend most of her time.

And what about Jane Hart? An airplane and helicopter pilot, mother of eight, and captain of her own sailboat, she was also a passionate activist, putting herself on the line for causes she believed in, even though it made her supportive husband's political advisers nervous. In 1967, she was arrested, along with hundreds of others, for participating in a peaceful protest of the Vietnam War at the Pentagon. When she showed up for her trial date, there were reporters everywhere. Hart was disappointed to discover that an act of civil disobedience attracted so much more attention than her congressional hearings had.

But Hart's high-profile position in those astronaut hearings had caught the attention of Betty Friedan, a leader in the emerging women's rights movement. When Friedan started the National Organization for Women, in 1966, she invited Hart to be one of the founders of that group. Hart happily accepted and opened two chapters, one in her home state of Michigan and one in Washington, D.C. Hart also heard from Liz Carpenter, with a request from then president Lyndon Johnson to put together a women's advisory group for the FAA. She led the Women's Advisory Committee on Aviation, on which B Steadman and Gene Nora Stumbough Jessen also served. Hart was living a full life—pilot, mother, and now key player in the women's rights movement. And on that front, there was much work to be done.

Chapter 11

We Want to See a Woman Driving the Bus, Not Sitting in the Back

Changing the "Social Order"

According to a *Ms.* magazine article published in 1973, "In 1967, seventeen women with advanced degrees in fields directly related to space" applied to the space program. They were not admitted. Women were still not welcomed into the astronaut corps. The only image that remotely associated *woman* and *astronaut* was the female model posing for the powdered drink mix Tang and reciting the line, "If it's good enough for the astronauts, it's good enough for my family."

Yet many of the things that women could not do in the 1960s—rent a car, get a loan, play team sports—began to be possible by the 1970s. More women were entering the fields of engineering and science, and women began graduating from medical schools in record numbers. In the 1960s, there were only ten women in Congress. By the 1970s, that number reached thirty-one. (In 2008, that number had climbed to ninety.)

The changes became obvious just by turning on the television. Gone was *Leave It to Beaver*, in which the wife greeted the husband with, "Well, the head of the house is home." In its place were shows like *Mary Tyler Moore*, which featured a single, working independent girl determined to "make it on her own," and *One Day at a Time*, which centered on a divorced career woman raising teenage girls by herself.

Mission specialist Sally Ride on the space shuttle *Challenger*'s middeck

Gloria Steinem shook up the women's movement in the 1970s and continues to fight for change today.

The media was reflecting how women were starting to be seen in the real world.

And in the real world, the women's liberation movement was in full swing. Betty Friedan's book *The Feminine Mystique,* published in 1963, had become a bestseller. The National Organization for Women was growing in strength and power. And another force to be reckoned with, Gloria Steinem, had joined the women's movement. Steinem founded *Ms.* magazine in 1972, empowering readers each month with a national publication dedicated to women's issues. By 1978, the Equal Pay Act—which said that employers could not discriminate against women by paying them less money than a man doing the same job—had been in effect for fifteen years and was starting to make a difference in the workplace.

These changes in the "social order" referred to by John Glenn in the subcommittee hearings began to have an effect on NASA. In 1976, the jet-test-pilot requirement was modified, and NASA created new ways for potential astronauts to join the program. The space agency announced that there were now two different types of astronaut jobs: pilots were on one track, mission and payload specialists on the other. To be a pilot, jet-test experience was now considered "highly desirable." It was not required at all for the other two positions. And women were finally invited to apply to be astronauts.

There's Space for Everyone

NASA may have anticipated being flooded with woman applicants that year. But it wasn't. There wasn't much of a response at all from women or minorities. It seemed that even though the credentials had changed and NASA was open to a larger pool of applicants, women and minorities had already decided that it wouldn't be worth their time to apply because of the reputation the agency had gained for discrimination. So NASA went out looking for female and minority candidates with a nationwide recruitment effort. The slogan: There's Space for Everyone.

The recruitment campaign featured Nichelle Nichols, the African-American actress who played *Star Trek*'s Lieutenant Uhura. Margaret Weitekamp said, "It's remarkable that when NASA was asked to come up with a vision of a mixed-sex, mixed-race space crew, the best one they could find was fictional. But it was successful. Mae Jemison [who became the first woman of color to go into space, in 1992] directly credits the campaign with her decision to apply."

Finally, in 1978, women were admitted to the space program for the first time.

Ride, Sally, Ride

Sally Ride was one of those women.

Sally Ride was also one of the women who had grown up in a nation that was looking at females differently from the way it had twenty years earlier—a nation much changed since Cobb was a girl.

All of this change affected not only the opportunities that women had in 1978 but also the mind-set with which they approached their lives. Sally Ride and the other women admitted into the astronaut class of 1978 had not grown up being told all the many things they could not do because they were girls. Instead, they had been allowed to dream.

And dream Ride did.

Her first dream was to become a professional tennis player. She was nationally ranked on the junior tournament circuit. She had always loved science and decided to study physics and astrophysics at Stanford University. Her next dream began as her academic career was ending. While finishing her doctoral degree work at Stanford, Ride read that NASA was accepting astronaut applicants. "I looked at the list of credentials and said, 'I'm one of those people.'" Ride was aware of the doors that had been opened for her. "The women's movement had already paved the way, I think, for my coming."

Sally Ride became the first American woman in space on June 18, 1983, when she flew as a mission specialist aboard *Challenger*.

No question, women had come a long way. There were 8,079 applicants to the program in 1978, and 1,544 of them were women. Of the thirty-five astronauts admitted, Sally Ride and five other women—Shannon Lucid, Judith Resnik, Kathryn Sullivan, Anna Fisher, and Margaret Rhea Seddon—were included.

They were astronauts, but there was still room for improvement. "Mission specialist" was a new position in the space program. Mission specialists are scientists and researchers. They are trained in everything but one thing—flying a spacecraft.

In 1978, the first six women were admitted to the space program. They are (left to right) Margaret R. "Rhea" Seddon, Kathryn D. Sullivan, Judith A. Resnick, Sally K. Ride, Anna L. Fisher, and Shannon W. Lucid. The "rescue ball" they are posing with was a prototype, created as a possible means of transporting astronauts from one shuttle to another in case of an emergency. It was never used on a mission.

None of the six women who were admitted applied as pilots. Neither did the four—and first—minority men, who were also admitted to that class. They were all mission specialists. Of course this doesn't take anything away from their accomplishments, but it does explain why the milestone didn't make a huge impression on some of the thirteen women who went through testing in 1961. They were all pilots. And they were still waiting for a female pilot to become an astronaut.

Jerri Truhill's reaction, as always, cut to the chase. While she was thrilled that women had been let into the program, she also said, "We want to see a woman driving the bus, not sitting in the back."

Sally Ride monitors control panels on STS-7. A flight procedures notebook floats in front of her.

Eileen Collins is both the first woman to pilot a space shuttle and the first woman to serve as a space shuttle commander.

Reaching that milestone would take NASA another two decades, but the ground-work was laid in the mid-1970s, when the military was desegregated. Without the military's letting women in, there would not have been any female military test pilots to even apply as pilot astronauts to NASA. It was the navy that led the way.

At this time, it looked as though the Equal Rights Amendment (ERA) was going to pass. This amendment stated that equality of rights could not be denied based on gender. Rather than waiting to be told what to do, Admiral Elmo Zumwalt got a jump on things and encouraged the navy to open flight training to women. The navy obliged in 1974, and the army and air force followed. Suddenly, women *could* be jet test pilots.

One of those women was Eileen Collins. Like the Lovelace women, Collins had wanted to fly since she was a little girl. After she graduated from college, she went into the air force and got her wings.

July 23, 1999

It had been sixteen years since Sally Ride went up. Once again, the number of positive portrayals of women on the small screen had grown and now included the out-spoken, opinionated news reporter in the lead role on *Murphy Brown,* two tough-as-nails New York City detectives on the drama *Cagney and Lacey,* a high-powered career woman who employed a male housekeeper on *Who's the Boss?,* and three young women, figuring life out for themselves alongside three male counterparts on *Friends.* On the big screen, the movie *Mr. Mom* featured a mother becoming her family's breadwinner after the father loses his job and their roles are reversed. Suddenly Daddy was dealing with diapers while Mommy was battling corporate America and outsmarting her male boss.

And back at Cape Canaveral, Eileen Collins was sitting in the left seat—the *driver's* seat—of the space shuttle *Columbia.*

She was the *commander.*

She was about to fly that shuttle.

Commander Collins checked the panels on the flight deck one last time and gave the all clear to radio control.

The eyes of the world were on her—the first woman ever to command a space shuttle.

Across the river from the launchpad, seven of our thirteen women watched from the bleachers.

The owner of the eighth pair of eyes was down in front of the pack, once again keeping to herself, perhaps wanting to keep the moment private. Jerrie Cobb paced back and forth. When the countdown clock reached T minus five seconds, she stopped pacing and sat down in the wet grass.

This time, there was no delay.

The rockets ignited.

A wall of flame.

The light was blinding.

The crowd began to yell. "Go, go, go!"

Our women may have yelled the loudest. Sheer joy came from their mouths in cheers for Eileen Collins.

The roar of the shuttle was deafening.

The earth rumbled like an earthquake had struck, triggering great rippling waves in the water that reflected the flames, making the water look as though it had turned to fire.

Then she was up.

The shuttle broke loose from the booster rockets.

She was up and on her way.

And then all was quiet.

An awed hush settled over the crowd like a blanket.

They watched until the shuttle was clear out of sight, tears streaming down their faces.

Jerrie had felt the earth shake similarly before—four years earlier, at Collins's first launch into space, as the first woman pilot of a shuttle. Jerrie had watched that spacecraft burst off the pad. She had watched it rocket up into the clear night sky. On that trip, Collins had carried with her a gold pin from Jerrie depicting a Colombian bird, the symbol of both Jerrie's airplane and her entire life. This time, with Jerrie staying behind once again on Earth, it was her hopes and dreams that went hurtling into space with Collins, along for the ride.

On July 23, 1999, the space shuttle *Columbia* took to the skies with Eileen Collins at the helm.

Chapter 12

I Am Living Proof That Dreams Do Come True

Women with Wings

Some may read the story of these thirteen women and think that their adventure did not have a happy ending. But that depends on where you draw the finish line. The women were stopped in 1962. But they confronted NASA, exposed the trap of the jet-pilot rule, and destroyed the idea that women could not handle stress as well as men. And then Sally Ride *did* fly, and Eileen Collins *did* command the shuttle. Today, women are flying into space. But women who want their wings still continue to battle prejudice. So women continue to find inspiration in the story of these thirteen pioneers. Here are some examples of challenges women still face and of the new beginnings that are taking place.

In July 2006, during the *Discovery* shuttle launch, CNN's Miles O'Brien gave the male astronauts lengthy and respectful coverage, highlighting their career achievements and skills. But when he switched to covering the female crew members, he mainly focused on how their children were holding up in their absence and wondered about the two women's hobbies. The website space.com also discussed the two women's hobbies and how their children might be feeling about Mom's mission. Somehow none of the discussions about the men ventured into this territory.

Today, women can be found in most, if not all, fields that used to be thought of as "male," but there is still a long way to go. Women hold only 25 percent of the

In 2007, astronaut Peggy Whitson (right) became the first commander of the International Space Station. Here, she greets astronaut Pam Melroy, STS-120 commander, at the October 25 hatch opening between the International Space Station and the space shuttle *Discovery*.

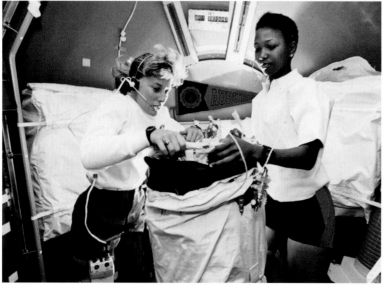

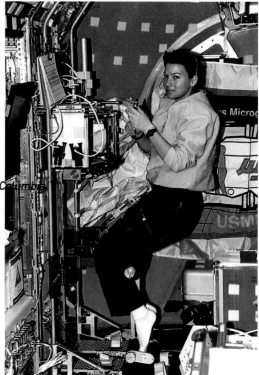

(Top) Kalpana Chawla is helped into her suit as she prepares to enter *Columbia* for launch; (left) Jan Davis and Mae Jemison work on board the STS-47; (right) Catherine Coleman works on board *Columbia* in the Spacelab science module. (Opposite) Susan Helms works outside the International Space Station with her feet anchored to the robotic arm on *Discovery*. In March 2001, it was the longest "walk" to date.

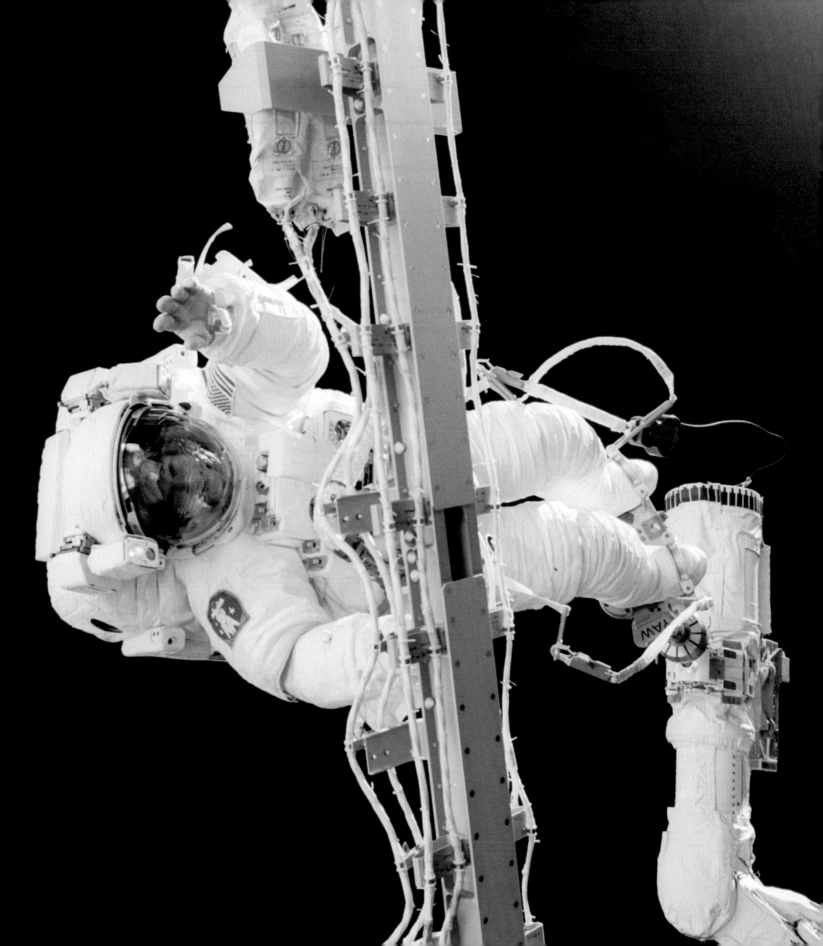

technology, science, and engineering jobs. Encouraging girls to continue their interest in science is a key factor in increasing the numbers of women in jobs such as the astronaut corps. In 2005, Ride said, "Today, the astronaut corps is almost 25 percent female, and I want that to continue to rise."

She is certainly doing her part to continue breaking down gender barriers. She started a company called Sally Ride Science, devoted to encouraging kids to pursue science. The company organizes science camps and festivals and produces publications for kids and parents.

The Sally Ride Science Festival, created by former astronaut Sally Ride, encourages and inspires girls to follow career paths in science, math, and technology.

Women Can Be Fighter Pilots

In March 2006, Captain Nicole Malachowski took to the skies, becoming the first woman Thunderbird pilot. The Thunderbirds are the best of the best the air force has to offer, elite fighter pilots who spend two years doing air shows in their F-16 jets as demonstration pilots. Some of the formations they fly in are so precise that the wingtip of one plane is only eighteen inches away from the next plane's wingtip!

Malachowski could be the poster child for how far this nation has come in empowering young girls to believe that they can do anything. Yet even this daring woman felt a small sting of discrimination growing up. When she was young, lying on her bed, staring up at a poster of the inside of a cockpit and dreaming about her future, women were still not allowed to be fighter pilots—and her male teacher told her so. Otherwise, however, she has had virtually no experience with gender barriers. "I think I am living proof that dreams do come true," she says.

There are some naysayers who show up at air shows from time to time to tell her that they think a woman can't cut it. How does she handle it? She tells them, "The proof is in the pudding. Watch the show. Point out which one's the girl." No one has ever been able to.

The air force lifted the ban on women becoming fighter pilots when Malachowski was a junior at the academy. When she found out about the change, she said to herself, "Wow, women can be fighter pilots, woo-hoo!" And then, she says, "It hit me—I ought to put my money where my mouth is!"

Becoming a fighter pilot is exactly what she did. Malachowski knows women paved the way. "You always stand on the shoulders of the people that came before you. I would not be here today if not for the likes of the 'Mercury 13,' no doubt about it."

Educating people about being a pilot in the air force is part of being a Thunderbird, and Malachowski talks to kids all the time. She sends a clear message. "I don't believe in barriers. . . . Do not become distracted from your goals by negative people or people who don't believe in your dreams as much as you. . . . Get rid of them and keep on going. . . . Just fly your plane."

About being the first female Thunderbird pilot, she said, "Someone had to go first. And the most wonderful thing is that I am the first and not the last. And that's what's important." She later said, "Women are going to add their strength and skills to the effort of pushing aviation forward."

Yet even though this is so, it is always an uphill battle to achieve equality and balance. It is wonderful that we can board a commercial jet these days and find a female

In 2006, air force jet pilot Nicole Malachowski became the first woman Thunderbird.

STS-83 crew members Mission Specialist Catherine Coleman, Pilot Susan Still, and Mission Specialist Janice Voss during their Terminal Countdown Demonstration Test in March 1997.

Commander Peggy Whitson floats in the Destiny laboratory on the International Space Station.

Mission Specialist Kathryn Sullivan poses for a picture before donning her space suit in the air lock of *Discovery*.

captain piloting it. But their numbers are small. According to 2007 FAA statistics, only 6 percent of all pilots are women. And that number falls when it comes to jets. To fly a jet, a pilot needs an airline transport rating, and only 3.5 percent of people holding those ratings are women. But not all pilots with transport ratings actually fly jets, so the estimated number of female jet pilots drops even further.

And why aren't there more women in the astronaut program? In 2007, Sally Ride said, "If you'd asked us twenty years ago, we would have expected there would be more women in the profession by now." Even though our culture embraces the idea that girls can do anything boys can do, fewer girls than boys pursue career paths that

In 2008, astronaut Sunita Williams was appointed NASA's deputy chief of the Astronaut Office. It is the most senior astronaut position at NASA.

(Following page) In 1999, ten of the women gathered at the Smithsonian Air and Space Museum. From left to right they are: Sarah Gorelick Ratley, Gene Nora Stumbough Jessen, Myrtle "K" Cagle, Jerrie Cobb, Irene Leverton, Jane Hart, Jerri Sloan Truhill, Rhea Hurrle Woltman, B Steadman, and Wally Funk.

require math and science. The most drastic change occurs in college, where more technical majors, such as computer science and electrical engineering, are increasingly being ruled out by female students. Are women still feeling the need to choose between motherhood and a career? Or is it more complicated than that? Eileen Collins, who fits her own description, says, "I want young women to know that you can get married and have children and be a pilot and an engineer."

In June 2007, the U.S. House of Representatives passed a resolution honoring the achievements of the thirteen women who paved the way for female astronauts who follow in their footsteps. Of these thirteen women, pilot-astronaut Pam Melroy said, "We enjoy a level of credibility, of respect and acceptance, that we would not have but for those women. And they fought every inch of the road ahead of us to enable us to enjoy what we have now."

It seems we are finally ready to acknowledge that there should be no Wrong Time for women with the Right Stuff. How can we help motivate young women to continue to strive for their dreams without letting anything get in their way? Role models such as these thirteen women help enormously. May their lights shine brightly on, illuminating the possibilities others can pursue.

Author's Note

When I first came across an obscure mention of a group of women often called the "Mercury 13," I was in the throes of doing research for a book about Ilan Ramon, Israel's first astronaut. The story caught my eye, but I was on deadline, so I filed it away for safekeeping. Not long after, and quite out of the blue, my dear friend and writer pal Sarah Aronson mentioned these women to me. She thought it was a story I might be interested in telling young readers. As soon as I could, I turned my attention to these women, and their story consumed me. But finding a way to tell it would prove elusive.

Theirs was a multidimensional story, peppered with many players and complicated by layers of history and politics. My initial idea was to write a collective picture-book biography profiling each woman. But that didn't work. It was way too much information for a picture book. I had written a poem for one of the women that I felt captured her essence as a young girl. That led me to wonder if I might introduce these women as they were when they were budding pilots, and I began to write more poems based on their lives. But that wasn't right either. It was too *little* information.

I soon realized that the picture-book format itself was what was holding me back. When I gave up trying to fit this colossal story into a picture book and just let the narrative flow, the manuscript started taking shape in both prose *and* poetry. Still, it was a hard sell. Editors told me it was "beautiful," but they weren't sure what to do with it. It didn't fit in any genre. Then I found an editor, Marc Aronson, who was able to help me see my vision more clearly. But the poetry was still problematic. Even when I tried to set off the poems in a gallery section paying tribute to each of these women, it did not flow well with the rest of the book. They had to come out. So I find myself feeling just as I would if I had had to cut a beloved character out of a novel. And although I have told the story of these women as I think it can best be told, I would love to share the poems with those of you who care to read them. They are available on both my personal website and Candlewick's website (www.candlewick.com). I hope you enjoy them and, for teachers, find them useful for class discussions. Most of all, they are another way in which I can honor all of these women for their accomplishments, their strength, and their adventurous spirits.

In thinking about these women as pioneers, I was led to *Webster's* dictionary, which defines the word *pioneer* as, "A person or group that originates or helps open up a new line of thought or activity." This describes these women perfectly. They *were* pioneers. They proved that women were equally prepared as men to be astronauts— and in some cases, were *better* suited than men. They challenged the prevailing ideas of what women were and were not allowed to do. They fought back when they were told no. They weakened barriers and poked holes in stereotypes. As with any group of people, they did not all hold the same opinions of what happened. And at the time, they did not have the opportunity to share their thoughts with one another. It was years before they met as a group, before there was a sense of unity among them. But they are bonded by a unique experience only they share. I count myself lucky to have had the good fortune of getting to know some of these wonderful women.

Telling this story changed my own writing. This was my first departure from what I would call my "straight" nonfiction. I had a successful career as an editor of children's nonfiction and had published many well-received books for the library market. But figuring out how to approach this story prompted me to reinvent the way I thought about writing and the way I thought about myself as a writer. It unlocked my creativity in new ways. And it became the first of several works with an emerging theme of strong women and girls. This is a theme that calls out to me time and again. The writing of this story preceded the writing of my debut novel about girls, as well as the writing of my debut picture-book biography about Elizabeth Cady Stanton, although both were released before this book. Looking back, I realize that writing this story was a pivotal moment in my life as a writer. It even affected certain parts of my nonwriting life.

While researching what happened to these thirteen women, I visited airfields. I talked to pilots. I took a lesson in a two-seater Cessna 152. I got to stand a hundred feet away from F-16 jets as they thundered past, and I even got to climb into one to get a close-up look at the equipment and learn how to strap into a pressure suit. Filling my senses with the sights, sounds, and smells of airplanes brought these women's stories alive for me. But nothing did more to educate me than getting to know the people involved. Certainly, the course of my research led me to many books, articles, scientific papers, audio recordings, and videotapes, but it also led me to many interesting people. I developed relationships and spent a considerable amount of time talking with museum curators, female aviators such as Betty Skelton and Nicole Malachowski, and Cathryn Walters Liberson, the scientist who helped conduct the isolation tests with the women. And, most thrilling, my research led me to the women themselves. There were e-mails, letters, phone calls, and even an incredible weekend spent with eight of them—Jerrie Cobb included. We chatted, we laughed, and we broke bread—what better way is there to get a sense of who people really are? It was during that weekend that Jerrie Cobb confided in me what really happened in that private office meeting with Lyndon B. Johnson.

In talking to several of these amazing ladies, I became infected by their contagious love of flying. More than one of them has encouraged me to get my private pilot's license. If I do get my wings, it will be because these women are a profound source of inspiration. They are true examples of how anyone—regardless of age, race, or gender—can pursue their dreams for their dreams' sake—no matter the outcome. Whether we ever have the gift of knowing it or not, we all play a part in paving the way for the forward motion of our world.

Appendix

In total, twenty-five women were invited to take the Lovelace tests. Nineteen of the invitees completed the tests, with thirteen passing them. Fran Bera and Patricia Jetton did not pass due to health issues the Lovelace team detected. In 1999, Fran Bera and Georgiana McConnell were among the honored female guests at the Eileen Collins launch.

The six who did not take the tests were as follows: Marilyn Link and Frances Miller did not accept the invitation, Link because she felt she was too old and was also in the midst of a career change, Miller because she did not believe the program would be successful. Dorothy Anderson and Sylvia Roth both accepted the invitation, but neither was able to get time off from work in order to take the tests. Marjorie Dufton and Elaine Harrison also agreed to take the tests, but neither did, for reasons that are not known.

Completed and Passed Tests	Completed Tests	Did Not Take Tests
Myrtle "K" Cagle	Frances "Fran" Bera	Dorothy Anderson
Jerrie Cobb	Virginia Holmes	Marjorie Dufton
Jan Dietrich	Patricia K. Jetton	Elaine Harrison
Marion Dietrich	Georgiana T. McConnell	Marilyn Link
Wally Funk	Joan Ann Meriam (Smith)	Frances Miller
Sarah Gorelick (Ratley)	Betty J. Miller	Sylvia Roth
Jane Hart		
Jean Hixson		
Rhea Hurrle (Woltman)		
Irene Leverton		
Jerri Sloan (Truhill)		
Bernice "B" Steadman		
Gene Nora Stumbough (Jessen)		

Source: Weitekamp, Margaret A. *Right Stuff, Wrong Sex: America's First Women in Space Program.* Baltimore: Johns Hopkins University Press, 2004. pp. 94–95.

Further Reading

Atkins, Jeannine. *Wings and Rockets: The Story of Women in Air and Space.* New York: Farrar, Straus and Giroux, 2003.

Borden, Louise, and Mary Kay Kroeger. *Fly High! The Story of Bessie Coleman.* New York: Margaret McElderry Books, 2001.

Cummins, Julie. *Tomboy of the Air: Daredevil Pilot Blanche Stuart Scott.* New York: HarperCollins, 2001.

———. *Women Daredevils: Thrills, Chills, and Frills.* New York: Dutton, 2008.

Ride, Sally, with Susan Okie. *To Space and Back.* New York: HarperCollins, 1989.

Ryan, Pam Muñoz. *Amelia and Eleanor Go for a Ride.* New York: Scholastic, 1999.

Stone, Tanya Lee. *Amelia Earhart.* New York: DK Publishing, 2007.

Thimmesh, Catherine. *Team Moon: How 400,000 People Landed Apollo 11 on the Moon.* Boston: Houghton, 2006.

Yolen, Jane. *My Brothers' Flying Machine: Wilbur, Orville, and Me.* New York: Little, Brown, 2003.

Webliography

The Ninety-Nines is the International Organization of Women Pilots. It was started by ninety-nine female pilots in 1929. Most of the "Mercury 13" women belonged to the Ninety-Nines. To learn more about this group, which is still going strong today, visit: http://www.museumofwomenpilots.com

The International Women's Air & Space Museum, in Cleveland, Ohio, was cofounded by B Steadman in 1986. There is a wonderful "Mercury 13" exhibit there. To visit the museum online, go to: http://www.iwasm.org

Women in Aviation is a great source for statistics and news about women in aviation: http://www.wai.org

To read biographies of many women astronauts, visit: http://info.uah.edu/colleges/liberal/womensstudies/astronauts.html

To visit an online NASA exhibit of Women's Achievements in Aviation and Space, go to: http://www.hq.nasa.gov/office/pao/women_gallery/sitemap.htm

The Texas Women's University has extensive information about women in aviation, focused on the Women's Airforce Service Pilots (WASP). http://www.twu.edu/library/wasp/index.htm

To learn more about Sally Ride Science, visit: http://www.sallyridescience.com

Sources

BOOKS

Ackmann, Martha. *The Mercury 13: The Untold Story of Thirteen American Women and the Dream of Space Flight.* New York: Random House, 2003.

Atkinson, Joseph D., Jr., and Jay M. Shafritz. *The Real Stuff: A History of NASA's Astronaut Recruitment Program.* New York: Praeger, 1985.

Bell, Elizabeth S. "Women Flyers: From Aviatrix to Astronaut." In *Heroines of Popular Culture,* edited by Pat Browne. Bowling Green, OH: Bowling Green State University Popular Press, 1987.

Boase, Wendy. *The Sky's the Limit: Women Pioneers in Aviation.* New York: Macmillan, 1979.

Cobb, Jerrie. *Jerrie Cobb: Solo Pilot.* Sun City Center, FL: Jerrie Cobb Foundation, 1997.

———, with Jane Rieker. *Woman Into Space: The Jerrie Cobb Story.* Englewood Cliffs, NJ: Prentice-Hall, 1963.

Dallek, Robert. *Flawed Giant: Lyndon Johnson and His Times, 1961–1973.* New York: Oxford University Press, 1998.

Douglas, Deborah G. *American Women and Flight Since 1940.* Lexington: University Press of Kentucky, 2004.

Douglas, Susan J. *Where the Girls Are: Growing Up Female with the Mass Media.* New York: Times Books/ Random House, 1994.

Freni, Pamela. *Space for Women: A History of Women with the Right Stuff.* Santa Ana, CA: Seven Locks Press, 2002.

Haynsworth, Leslie, and David Toomey. *Amelia Earhart's Daughters: The Wild and Glorious Story of American Women Aviators from World War II to the Dawn of the Space Age.* New York: William Morrow, 1998.

Inness, Sherrie A. *Tough Girls: Women Warriors and Wonder Women in Popular Culture.* Philadelphia: University of Pennsylvania Press, 1999.

Jessen, Gene Nora. *The Powder Puff Derby of 1929: The First All Women's Transcontinental Air Race.* Sourcebooks, 2002.

Kevles, Bettyann Holtzmann. *Almost Heaven: The Story of Women in Space.* New York: Basic Books, 2003.

Klein, Allison. *What Would Murphy Brown Do? How the Women of Prime Time Changed Our Lives.* Emeryville, CA: Seal Press, 2006.

Moolman, Valerie. *Women Aloft.* Alexandria, VA: Time-Life Books, 1981.

Nolen, Stephanie. *Promised the Moon: The Untold Story of the First Women in the Space Race.* Toronto: Penguin Canada, 2002.

Rich, Doris L. *Jackie Cochran: Pilot in the Fastest Lane.* Gainesville: University Press of Florida, 2007.

Spigel, Lynn, and Denise Mann, eds. *Private Screenings: Television and the Female Consumer.* Minneapolis: University of Minnesota Press, 1992.

Steadman, Bernice Trimble. *Tethered Mercury: A Pilot's Memoir: The Right Stuff—but the Wrong Sex.* Traverse City, MI: Aviation Press, 2001.

Weibel, Kathryn. *Mirror, Mirror: Images of Women Reflected in Popular Culture.* Garden City, NY: Anchor Books, 1977.

Weitekamp, Margaret A. *Right Stuff, Wrong Sex: America's First Women in Space Program.* Baltimore: Johns Hopkins University Press, 2004.

Wolfe, Tom. *The Right Stuff.* New York: Farrar, Straus and Giroux, 1979.

Yellin, Emily. *Our Mothers' War: American Women at Home and at the Front During World War II.* New York: Free Press, 2004.

ARTICLES AND DOCUMENTS

Ackmann, Martha. "Space Invaders." *Salon,* July 27, 2000. http://dir.salon.com/story/mwt/feature/tues/2000/06/27/astronauts

"The Astronauts—Ready to Make History." *Life,* September 14, 1959.

Bisbee, Dana. "Pilot Wants Her Shot in Space." *Boston Herald,* August 28, 1998.

Brown, Erika. "Sending Your Daughters to Space." *Forbes,* October 5, 2005.

Burbank, Sam. "Mercury 13's Wally Funk Fights for Her Place in Space." *National Geographic Today,* July 9, 2003.

Carpenter, Liz. Letter drafted for Vice President Lyndon B. Johnson to send to James Webb, dated March 15, 1962. LBJ Library.

———. Memorandum to Vice President Lyndon B. Johnson, March 14, 1962. LBJ Library.

Cobb, Jerrie. Letter to Vice President Lyndon B. Johnson, April 17, 1962. LBJ Library.

———. Letter to the FLATS, April 13, 1962. International Women's Air and Space Museum.

———. Letter to the FLATS, August 15, 1962. International Women's Air and Space Museum.

———. Letter to the FLATS, August 22, 1962. International Women's Air and Space Museum.

———. "Space for Women?" Speech presented at the First Women's Space Symposium, Los Angeles, February 22, 1962.

———.Telegram to Bernice Trimble Steadman, July 18, 1962, 6:36 p.m.

———. with Jane Rieker. "Hopeful Astronaut Leaps Tilt and Tank Test Hurdle." *Daily Oklahoman,* July 18, 1963.

Cochran, Jacqueline. Letter to Bernice Steadman (with copies sent to the eleven other "Mercury 13" women), July 12, 1961. International Women's Air and Space Museum.

———. Letter to Jerrie Cobb, March 23, 1962. International Women's Air and Space Museum.

———. "Women in Space: Famed Aviatrix Predicts Women Astronauts within Six Years." *Parade,* April 30, 1961.

Cox, Donald. "Woman Astronauts." *Space World,* September 1961.

"Damp Prelude to Space." *Life,* October 24, 1960.

Davis, Verla D. "Becoming Thunderbird Is Dream Come True for Nevada Native." U.S. Air Forces in Europe News Service, July 7, 2005. http://www.f-16.net/news_article1411.html.

Dietrich, Marion. "First Woman into Space." *McCall's,* September 1961.

Donnelly, Francis X. "Pioneer Flier Shoots for Stars, Bids for Spaceflight." *Florida Today,* June 21, 1968.

Dunn, Marcia. "Female Flier Still Seeks Trip into Space." Associated Press, July 11, 1998.

Gadebusch, Ruth. "Women Still Wait for Chance in Outer Space." *Fresno Bee,* July 12, 2003.

Feldman, Claudia. "Shoulders to Stand On: Mercury 13 Pioneered the Way for Female Astronauts." *Houston Chronicle,* July 1, 2003.

"Foiled Astronaut." *New York Times,* June 26, 1983.

"From Aviatrix to Astronautrix." *Time,* August 29, 1960.

Hart, Jane. "Women in Orbit." *Town and Country,* November 1962.

Hoffstetter, Jane. "She'd Be First Woman in Space." *Fort Lauderdale News,* May 19, 1961.

"I'm One of Those People." *New York Times,* June 18, 1983.

Johnson, Lyndon B. Letter to Mrs. Catherine Smith, March 24, 1962. LBJ Library.

———. Letter to Mrs. George B. Ward, March 24, 1962. LBJ Library.

Kocivar, Ben. "The Lady Wants to Orbit." *Look,* February 2, 1960.

Kozloski, Lillian, and Maura J. Mackowski. "The Wrong Stuff." *Final Frontier,* May/June 1990.

Krum, Sharon. "Space Cowgirl." *Guardian,* April 2, 2002.

Laboda, Amy. "The 'Mercury 13': Were They the First Ladies of Space?" *AOPA Pilot,* February 1997.

Larlee, Staff Sgt. Jeremy. "Face of Defense: Women's Aviation Hall of Fame Inducts Air Force Pilot." Air Force News Agency, March 19, 2008.

"A Lady Proves She's Fit for Space Flight." *Life,* August 29, 1960.

Latty, Yvonne. "Cobb Using Glenn's Latest flight to Renew Her Space Dreams." Knight Ridder/Tribune News Service, November 11, 1998, p. K2252.

Laughlin, Meg. "The Discarded Astronaut." *Miami Herald,* June 12, 1983.

Leverton, Irene. "Fire Fighter Aloft." *Woman Pilot* 10, no. 3 (May/June 2002).

Levine, Bettijane. "After 36 Years, She's Still Aiming for the Stars." *Los Angeles Times,* October 29, 1998.

Luce, Clare Boothe. "But Some People Simply Never Get the Message." *Life,* June 28, 1963.

McCarthy, Sheryl. "The Women of Mercury 13." *USA Today,* May 10, 2007.

McCullough, Joan. "The 13 Astronauts Who Were Left Behind." *Ms.,* September 1973.

Merzer, Martin. "'Mercury 13' Women Missed Their Chance to Blast Off." *Miami Herald,* October 23, 1998.

Nolen, Stephanie. "One Giant Leap—Backward." *Globe and Mail,* October 12, 2002.

NPR. "What Happened to the Mercury 13?" Science Friday Kids' Connection, Hour Two, June 20, 2003.

Oberg, James. "The Mercury 13: Setting the Story Straight." *Space Review,* May 14, 2007.

"One Hundred of the Most Important Young Men and Women in the United States." *Life,* September 14, 1962.

Peirce, Kate. "What if the Energizer Bunny Were Female? Importance of Gender in Perceptions of Advertising Spokes-character Effectiveness." *Sex Roles: A Journal of Research,* December 2001.

Precker, Michael. "Gender Grounded 13 Women with 'The Right Stuff.'" *Dallas Morning News,* October 11, 1998.

Qualifications for Astronauts: Hearings before the Special Subcommittee on the Selection of Astronauts, Committee on Science and Astronautics. U.S. House of Representatives, Eighty-seventh Congress, second session, July 17 and 18, 1962.

Qualifications for Astronauts: Report of the Special Subcommittee on the Selection of Astronauts, Committee on Science and Astronautics. U.S. House of Representatives, Eighty-seventh Congress, second session, serial S.

Rieker, Jane. "Up and Up Goes Jerrie Cobb." *Sports Illustrated,* August 29, 1960.

Rogers, Patrick. "Stargazer." *People,* October 19, 1998.

Ross, Sid. "My 7 Hours Out of This World." *Parade,* April 16, 1961.

Sellers, Laurin. "NASA at Last Honors 13 Women with the Right Stuff." *South Florida Sun-Sentinel,* May 23, 2004.

"Seven Brave Women Behind the Astronauts." *Life,* September 21, 1959.

Shurley, Jay T. "Profound Experimental Sensory Isolation." December 1960.

Shurley, Jay, and Cathryn Walters. Subject no. 52, concomitant recording (transcription of the audio recording from Jerrie Cobb's stint in the isolation tank).

———. Transcription of the audio recordings from Subjects B and C (Rhea Hurrle and Wally Funk) in the isolation tank.

———. "Woman Astronaut Assessment in the Hydrohypodynamic Environment." August 8, 1961.

Smith, Catherine. Letter to Vice President Lyndon B. Johnson, March 15, 1962. LBJ Library.

Smith, Jack. "The Craftier Sex Is Cleared for Space." *Los Angeles Times,* August 28, 1960.

"Stars in Their Eyes." *People,* July 7, 2003.

Steadman, Bernice Trimble. "Farewell to a Friend." IWASM Quarterly. 6, no. 1 (1992).

———. "Bernice T. Steadman and the Women in Space Program." B. Steadman Papers, IWASM.

Stevens, William K. "Feminism Paved Astronaut's Way." *New York Times,* May 2, 1982.

"12 Women to Take Astronaut Test." *New York Times,* January 26, 1961.

"The Unlucky Mercury 13." BBC News, July 13, 2003.

Walters, Cathryn, Jay T. Shurley, and Oscar A. Parsons. "Differences in Male and Female Responses to Underwater Sensory Deprivation: An Exploratory Study. *Journal of Nervous and Mental Disease* 135, no. 4 (1962), pp. 302–310.

Ward, Mrs. George B. Letter to Vice President Lyndon B. Johnson, received March 19, 1962. LBJ Library.

Weitekamp, Margaret A. "The 'Astronautrix' and the 'Magnificent Male': Jerrie Cobb's Quest to Be the First Woman in America's Manned Space Program." In *Impossible to Hold: Women and Culture in the 1960s,* Avital H. Bloch and Lauri Umansky, eds. New York: New York University Press, 2005, pp. 9–28.

"Woman Astronaut Ban Decried." *Women's Journal,* June 23, 1963.

"Woman Astronaut Predicted." *New York Times,* June 26, 1962.

"A Woman Passes Tests Given to 7 Astronauts." *New York Times,* August 19, 1960.

"Women Adaptable to Isolation, Tests Show." *Post and Times-Star,* December 6, 1961.

"Women as Astronauts." *New York Times,* March 16, 1962.

"Women Secretly Trained as U.S. Astronauts in 1960s." CNN, June 23, 2003.

"Would-Be Female Astronauts Honored by Wisconsin University." Aero-News Network, May 10, 2007.

VIDEO

In Search of History: *Mercury 13: The Secret Astronauts.* A&E Television, 1998. The History Channel.

James, Sara. Weekend Magazine, *Dateline* NBC.

Jennings, Peter. "A Closer Look: Beyond the Horizon." ABC news report, October 26, 1998.

Leave It to Beaver. Episode 96: "Beaver's Library Book."

"The Tank." WKY-TV, Oklahoma City, 1960.

Source Notes

Chapter 1

p. 5: "Go, Eileen! Go for all of us!" Author correspondence with Wally Funk, November 2007.

p. 5: "T minus six seconds!" and "Try T minus thirty-eight years." Ackmann, p. 192.

Chapter 2

p. 8: "But it was not bravery . . . challenge of this stuff." Wolfe, pp. 17, 21.

p. 12: "She is just a petite . . . than men," "a flat-chested lightweight . . . married," and "scientist-wife of a pilot": Kocivar, *Look*.

p. 12: "Women in space? . . . all out there!" Author correspondence with Betty Skelton, June 10, 2007.

p. 13: "I felt it was an opportunity . . . do it well." Weitekamp, p. 69.

p. 13: "I put in a very strong urge . . . 'Under no circumstances.'" Weitekamp, p. 71.

p. 13: "girl astronaut program": Ackmann, p. 46.

pp. 14–15: "No airline passenger . . . in the cockpit." Nolen, p. 57.

p. 15: "Honey, it's no career . . . a chance." Nolen, pp. 52–53.

p. 15: "I jumped at the offer." Hoffstetter, *Fort Lauderdale News*.

p. 16: "It's the lung-power . . . on a scale." Cobb, with Rieker, *Woman Into Space*, p. 139.

p. 18: "Here's the chicken switch." Cobb, with Rieker, *Daily Oklahoman*.

p. 18: "At five, I'd been given . . . far greater." Cobb, with Rieker, *Woman Into Space*, p. 143.

p. 19: "successfully completed . . . project": Ackmann, p. 69.

p. 19: "We are already in a position . . . male colleague" and "no definite space project . . . women": Weitekamp, in Bloch and Umansky.

p. 19: felt as if she headed the FBI's "most wanted" list: Cobb, with Rieker, *Woman Into Space*, p. 156.

p. 20: "The scientists . . . sex has come." Smith, Jack, *Los Angeles Times*.

p. 20: "[That] has nothing . . . about them." James, *Dateline* NBC.

p. 20: "Reporter: Do you think . . . I wouldn't say that." In Search of History: *Mercury 13, The Secret Astronauts.*

p. 20: "has never had a plan . . . future": Ackmann, p. 79.

pp. 20–21: "The consensus . . . of value." Weitekamp, p. 75.

p. 21: "One of the major objectives . . . fit the girls." Weitekamp, p. 76.

Chapter 3

p. 25: "I didn't know it was possible to be so alone." "The Tank."

p. 25: "I honestly believe . . . flat out die!" Ackmann, p. 111.

p. 25: ready to be alone with herself. Cobb, with Rieker, *Woman Into Space*, p. 167.

pp. 25–27: "All set," "Just . . . fine," "I find . . . like it," "Everything's fine . . . very peaceful," "There's some light . . . by the door," "Reporting in again . . . peaceful," and "I'll think I'll get out . . . stay in longer." Shurley and Walters, tank test transcription.

p. 27: "Two or two thirty p.m." Cobb, with Rieker, *Woman Into Space*, p. 173.

p. 27: "Probably not . . . Extraordinary." Cobb, with Rieker, *Woman Into Space*, p. 174.

p. 29: *"NOT a meaningful test!"* Ackmann, p. 103.

p. 31: "green and pressed the red 'chicken switch'": Freni, p. 52.

p. 31: "Are you ready?" "Yes," "twisting . . . time," and "was a dizzying blur": Cobb, with Rieker, *Woman Into Space*, pp. 151–152.

Chapter 4

p. 35: "When I was twenty-one . . . 'Whoa, I've got to do that.'" Laboda, *AOPA Pilot*.

p. 35: "There was an article . . . wrote to them." Laboda, *AOPA Pilot*.

p. 35: "So, I wrote Dr. Lovelace . . . without me." Weitekamp, p. 99.

p. 35: "I was never told . . . that's all." Laboda, *AOPA Pilot*.

p. 36: "Will you . . . candidate?" "I stumbled to a chair and fell into it," and "In stunned disbelief . . . unless you so desire." Dietrich, *McCall's*.

p. 37: Passengers might be nervous . . . as their pilot." Laboda, *AOPA Pilot*.

p. 38: "See, if the word got out . . . to starve." Nolen, pp. 158–159.

p. 38: "ratty-looking": Nolen, p. 168.

p. 38: "be up at 5:30 . . . all day long": Dietrich, *McCall's*.

p. 38: "volunteering for the initial examinations for female astronaut candidates" and "Mommy's going to the moon!" Ackmann, p. 74.

p. 39: "You were carrying everybody else on your shoulders." Ackmann, p. 95.

p. 39: "You're really in for it . . . stayin', too.'" Dietrich, *McCall's*.

p. 39: "Come with . . . every day" and "Try not to . . . electroencephalogram." Dietrich, *McCall's*.

p. 39: "combine a saint-like discipline with an unholy determination": Nolen, p. 173.

p. 40: "Well, here we are . . . through this thing." Nolen, p. 177.

p. 40: "Lovelace cocktail hour": Weitekamp, p. 106.

p. 40: "a million needles . . . arm and hand": Steadman, B Steadman papers, IWASM.

p. 42: "We never stopped . . . they hurt us." Nolen, p. 171.

p. 42: "You want an astronaut . . . give you one." Nolen, p. 171.

p. 43: "we collectively . . . by NASA": Nolen, p. 171.

p. 43: "Is that what they might use you for?" "Let the scientists dig up their own women," and "But I was thinking of asking you to marry me." Dietrich, *McCall's*.

Chapter 5

p. 46: "scratched, bruised, and breathless": Cobb, with Rieker, *Woman Into Space*, p. 196.

p. 46: "If you don't know . . . the project." Cobb, with Rieker, *Woman Into Space*, p. 197.

p. 47: "slowly maneuvering . . . the pool": Cobb, with Rieker, *Woman Into Space*, p. 198.

p. 50: "I was actually . . . to be true." Cobb, with Rieker, *Woman Into Space*, p. 201.

p. 50: "a great asset to any part of the program": Weitekamp, p. 124.

p. 50: "recommended that . . . by NASA": Cobb, with Rieker, *Woman Into Space*, p. 203.

p. 51: "If you kept your wits about you . . . to come out." Nolen, p. 200.

p. 51: "very minimal": Walters, Shurley, and Parsons, *Journal of Nervous and Mental Diseases.*

Chapter 6

p. 54: "The more extreme reaction . . . the pity for them." Hart, *Town and Country.*

p. 54: "I don't think they ever . . . a woman along." Atkinson, p. 94.

p. 55: "The Navy has canceled the tests," "What happened?" and "I don't know . . . I can tell you." Cobb, with Rieker, *Woman Into Space*, pp. 208–209.

p. 56: *"Regret to advise . . . W Randolph Lovelace II MD."* Ackmann, p. 132.

p. 56: "I still can't get over . . . Sunday morning flight," "I felt terrible . . . talk about it," and "I felt pure panic— I had no job!" Laboda, *AOPA Pilot.*

p. 56: "Sending a woman . . . desired." Weitekamp, p. 121.

p. 57: "to make a small roar": Ackmann, p. 136.

Chapter 7

p. 59: "Still nothing new to report . . . of the year." Postcard from K Cagle to Jerrie Cobb, IWASM.

p. 59: "The future use of women . . . to be astronauts." Cobb, with Rieker, *Woman Into Space*, p. 211.

p. 60: "Under the circumstances . . . had in mind." Weitekamp, p. 132.

p. 60: "the skills and imagination . . . sought in this vital area": Weitekamp, p. 133.

p. 60: "The race for space . . . for women!" Cobb, "Space for Women?"

pp. 60–61: "Just as in the past fifty years . . . in the space age." Hart, *Town and Country.*

p. 61: "and, of course, no women, thank you": Weitekamp, p. 121.

p. 62: "I think you could get . . . some encouragement" and "Do you think you could write . . . before they leave." Carpenter, Memorandum.

p. 62: "I'm sure you agree . . . orbital flight." Carpenter, Letter.

p. 62: *"Let's Stop This Now!"* and *"File."* Weitekamp, p. 90.

p. 63: "Why don't we put the first nonwhite man in space?" Haylesworth, pp. 230–231.

p. 65: "Both organizations . . . concerns outright." Weitekamp, p. 127.

p. 65: "We would like to urge you . . . things we can do." Ward, Letter.

p. 65: "I welcome your letter . . . with men." Johnson, Letter to Mrs. George B. Ward.

Chapter 8

pp. 67–70: Hearing description and quotations: Qualifications for Astronauts, hearing transcripts.

p. 72: "I'll take that bicycle test Monday" and "I can take some . . . Tuesday morning." Weitekamp, p. 80.

p. 72: "You might become the first woman astronaut who really earns that name." Cochran, *Parade*.

p. 72: "a properly organized . . . would be a fine thing": Cochran, Letter to Bernice Steadman.

p. 73: "Yes, I certainly am, but Jerrie hasn't told us when" and "Jerrie! . . . I'm heading this up!" Author interview with Jerri Sloan Truhill, April 2, 2007.

p. 73: "Jerrie Cobb isn't running this program. I am!" Ackmann, p. 83.

pp. 73–74: "due to marriage, childbirth, and other causes," "Miss Cochran . . . space program?" and "I certainly think . . . tell you afterward." Qualifications for Astronauts, hearing transcripts.

Chapter 9

pp. 77–82: Hearing description, quotations, and notes from Cobb and Cochran: Qualifications for Astronauts, hearing transcripts.

p. 82: "It didn't matter . . . women in this program." In Search of History: *Mercury 13: The Secret Astronauts.*

p. 82: "In the recent congressional hearing . . . was just childish." Hart, *Town and Country.*

p. 82: "It is inconceivable . . . restricted to men." Hart, *Town and Country.*

p. 82: "The guys didn't want us . . . a bunch of women." Laboda, *AOPA Pilot.*

p. 84: "The other thing . . . didn't complain as much." In Search of History: *Mercury 13: The Secret Astronauts.*

p. 84: "She told me I was her role model" and "The first thing . . . What happened?'" Bisbee, *Boston Herald.*

p. 85: "I think we all look forward . . . personification of the home." Weitekamp, p. 159.

Chapter 10

p. 87: "NASA never had any intention . . . before their time." Laboda, *AOPA Pilot.*

p. 89: "I had to give up many things . . . looking for adventure." Freni, p. 118.

p. 91: "share of shaking": Cobb, with Rieker, *Woman Into Space,* p. 221.

p. 92: "Likely first . . . candidates." "The Astronauts—Ready to Make History," *Life,* p. 4

Chapter 11

p. 95: "In 1967 . . . related to space," "If it's good enough . . . my family": McCullough, Joan, *Ms.*

pp. 96–97: "It's remarkable that when NASA . . . her decision to apply." Author correspondence with Margaret Weitekamp, July 19, 2007.

p. 97: "I looked at the list . . . those people' " and "The women's movement . . . my coming." Stevens, *New York Times.*

p. 98: "We want to see a woman . . . in the back." Ackmann, p. 185.

Chapter 12

p. 108: "Today, the astronaut corps . . . continue to rise." Brown, *Forbes.*

p. 109: "I think I am living proof that dreams do come true." Davis, U.S. Air Forces in Europe News Service.

p. 109: "The proof is in the pudding . . . one's the girl," "Wow, women can be . . . money where my mouth is!" "You always stand on . . . no doubt about it," "I don't believe in barriers . . . Just fly your plane," and "Someone had to go first . . . what's important." Author interview with Nicole Malachowski, August 11, 2006.

p. 109: "Women are going . . . aviation forward." Larlee, Air Force News Agency.

pp. 114–115: "If you'd asked us . . . by now" and "I want young women . . . and engineer." McCarthy, *USA Today.*

p. 115: "We enjoy a level of credibility . . . we have now." In Search of History: *Mercury 13: The Secret Astronauts.*

Photography Credits

p. i, ii–iii
NASA/Kennedy Space Center (NASA/KSC)

pp. vi–vii, viii–ix
© Image Farm Inc.

pp. x, 3, 4, 5
NASA/Kennedy Space Center (NASA/KSC)

p. 6   NASA/Marshall Space Flight Center (NASA/MSFC)

p. 8   Courtesy of NASA

p. 9   The National Archives

p. 10   The Woman's Collection, Texas Woman's University

p. 11   Courtesy of NASA

p. 12   Courtesy of Betty Skelton

p. 13   Courtesy of the International Women's Air & Space Museum

p. 15   © Ralph Crane/Time & Life Pictures/Getty Images

p. 16   © Carl Iwasaki/Time & Life Pictures/Getty Images

pp. 17–20
(all images) © Ralph Crane/Time & Life Pictures/Getty Images

p. 21   ("...And Boy Do I Need a Shave!") Jim Lange, © August 20, 1960, the *Daily Oklahoman*

p. 22   © A.Y. Owen/Time & Life Pictures/Getty Images

p. 26   © A.Y. Owen/Time & Life Pictures/Getty Images

p. 28   (all images) Courtesy of the Everett Collection

p. 32   NASA/Glenn Research Center (NASA/GRC), photograph by Arden Wilfong

p. 33   NASA/Glenn Research Center (NASA/GRC)

p. 34   Courtesy of the estate of Jean Hixson/Pauline Vincent

p. 36   Courtesy of the Museum of Women Pilots

p. 37   (both images) Courtesy of the Museum of Women Pilots

p. 38   The Woman's Collection, Texas Woman's University

p. 40   Courtesy of the International Women's Air & Space Museum

p. 41   (both images) Courtesy of the Lovelace Respiratory Research Institute, Gene Nora Jessen, and Jane Hart

p. 43   Courtesy of the International Women's Air & Space Museum

p. 44   Courtesy of NASA

p. 46   (both images) © Bill Bridges/Time & Life Pictures/Getty Images

p. 48   (all images) Official U.S. Navy photographs courtesy of National Museum of Naval Aviation

p. 51   Courtesy of Rhea Hurrle Woltman and Marilyn Hurrle

p. 52   Courtesy of the International Women's Air & Space Museum

p. 57   © Vincent D'Addario; The Mount Holyoke College Archives and Special Collections

p. 58   Courtesy of the United States Air Force

p. 61   NASA/Langley Research Center (NASA/LaRC)

p. 64   Courtesy of Lyndon Baines Johnson Library and Museum

p. 66   Library of Congress

p. 71   Courtesy of Air Force Flight Test Center History Office

p. 74   The Woman's Collection, Texas Woman's University

p. 76   © Douglas Martin/Pix Inc./Time Life Pictures/Getty Images

p. 78   Courtesy of NASA

p. 80   ("Two-Rocket Pads") Jim Lange, © July 19, 1962, the *Daily Oklahoman*

p. 81   Courtesy of the International Women's Air & Space Museum

p. 83   Courtesy of NASA

p. 84   ("Space Suffragette") Jim Lange, © July 27, 1962, the *Daily Oklahoman*

p. 85   Keystone/Getty Images/Hulton Archive

p. 86   Courtesy of the International Women's Air & Space Museum

p. 88   The Woman's Collection, Texas Woman's University

p. 89   Courtesy of the estate of Jean Hixson/Pauline Vincent

p. 90   Courtesy of Gene Nora Jessen

p. 91   Courtesy of the *Michigan Daily,* photograph by David Katz

p. 92   (left) © Howard Sochurek/Time & Life Pictures/Getty Images, (right) © A. Y. Owen/Time & Life Pictures/Getty Images

p. 94   Courtesy of NASA/Johnson Space Center

p. 96   © Yale Joel/Time Life Pictures/Getty Images

p. 98   Courtesy of NASA/Johnson Space Center

p. 99   Courtesy of NASA

p. 100 NASA/Glenn Research Center (NASA/GRC)

p. 103 NASA/Kennedy Space Center (NASA/KSC)

p. 104 Courtesy of NASA

p. 106 (top) NASA/Kennedy Space Center (NASA/KSC), (left, right) NASA/Marshall Space Flight Center (NASA/MSFC)

p. 107 NASA/Marshall Space Flight Center (NASA/MSFC)

p. 108 NASA/Kennedy Space Center (NASA/KSC)

pp. 110, 111
Courtesy of the United States Air Force

p. 112 NASA/Kennedy Space Center (NASA/KSC)

pp. 113,114
Courtesy of NASA

p. 115 NASA/Glenn Research Center (NASA/GRC)

pp. 116–117
Photograph by Michael Althaus

Index

airborne electroencephalogram (EEG) test, 46–47
airborne survival test, 49
airplane pilots, 2, 14–15, 37–38, 112, 114
    jet test pilots, 7, 8, 61, 65, 69, 70, 79, 101
    Thunderbird pilots, 109–111
    Women's Airforce Service Pilots (WASP), 2, 9, 10, 21, 39, 69,
        74, 75, 88
    See also individual pilots
altitude-chamber test, 46, 47
Anfuso, Victor, 65, 67, 68, 69, 70, 75, 77, 81
Ashby, Jeffrey S., 4

Ball, Lucille, 28, 29

Cagle, Myrtle "K.," 35, 36, 56, 59, 62, 86–87, 90, 115, 116–117
Carpenter, Liz, 61–62, 64, 65, 93
Carpenter, Scott, 6–7, 12, 14, 76–81, 87
Chawla, Kalpana, 106
Cobb, Jerrie, 35, 36, 49, 84, 115, 116–117
    Cochran against, 72–73, 74
    at congressional hearings, 66–70, 73–75, 81–82
    isolation tank test, 22–27, 29
    life after testing, 91–93
    Lyndon Johnson and, 62–63
    in MASTIF, 30, 31–33
    as NASA consultant, 50, 54, 55, 57, 59–65
    phase-one testing of, 14–21, 43
    phase-three testing of, 45–49
    phase-two testing of, 22–27, 29–30
    at shuttle launch, 1, 2, 102
Cochran, Jackie, 70–75, 82, 83
Coleman, Catherine G., 4, 106, 112
Collins, Eileen, 1–5, 100, 101–102, 105, 115
congressional hearings, 66–70, 73–82
Cox, Hiden T., 59

Daily Oklahoman, 21, 80, 84
Davis, Jan, 106
Dietrich, Jan, 36, 37, 39, 52–53, 72, 90
Dietrich, Marion, 36, 37, 39, 43, 52–53, 54, 72, 90
Dilbert Dunker test, 47–49
discrimination, 14–15, 37–38, 43, 62–65, 88, 90, 96, 105, 108–109
Douglas, Deborah, 82

Earhart, Amelia, v, 13
Equal Rights Amendment (ERA), 101

First National Conference on the Peaceful Uses of Space, 49
First Women's Space Symposium, 60–61
Fisher, Anna, 97–98

Flickinger, Donald, 13, 14, 15–16, 20–21, 53
Friedan, Betty, 93, 96
Funk, Wally, 2, 5, 35, 37, 51, 86–88, 115, 116–117

Glenn, John, 6–7, 12, 14, 29, 76–81, 87, 93, 96
Gorelick, Sarah, 2, 38, 53, 62, 72, 90, 115, 116–117

Hart, Jane, 2, 38, 39, 40, 54, 60–61, 91, 93, 115, 116–117
    at congressional hearings, 66–70, 73–75, 80, 81, 82
    Lyndon Johnson and, 61–65
    testing of, 40, 41
Hawley, Steven A., 4
Helms, Susan, 106
Hixson, Jean, 34–35, 39, 51, 88, 89
Hurrle, Rhea, 2, 37, 50–51, 56, 62, 91, 115, 116–117

International Space Station, 104–107, 112–113
International Women's Air and Space Museum, 86–87, 88, 90
isolation tank test, 22–27, 29, 51

Jemison, Mae, 97, 106
Jessen, Gene Nora Stumbough. *See* Gene Nora Stumbough
jet test pilots, 7, 8, 61, 65, 69, 70, 79, 101
Johnson, Lyndon B., 8, 61–65, 80

Kennedy, John F., 7, 8, 38, 56, 58–59, 60, 78
Kilgore, Donald, 84

Leverton, Irene, 2, 36, 38, 43, 53, 62, 89, 115, 116–117
Life magazine, 7, 8–9, 19–20, 35, 50, 53, 72, 91–92
Look magazine, 11–12
Lovelace, Randolph, 11, 13, 56, 57, 70, 84
    astronaut testing by, 14–21, 35–36, 43, 45, 49, 54–55
    and Jackie Cochran, 71, 72, 73, 82
    on test results, 49–50
Low, George, 77, 80, 82
Lucid, Shannon, 97–98

Malachowski, Nicole, 109–111
MASTIF (multiple-axis space test inertia facility), 30, 31–33
McCall's magazine, 54
Melroy, Pam, 104–105, 115
Mercury 7, v, 6–7, 10, 39–40, 76–77
    Betty Skelton and, 12
    Lovelace and, 11, 13, 16
    resistance to women as astronauts, 54, 61
    testing of, compared to Lovelace testing, 12, 18, 20, 25, 29,
        30, 31, 54
Miller, George, 65

minorities, 62–65, 96–97
mission specialists, 3–4, 94–95, 97–98, 112, 114
Ms. magazine, 95, 96
Murrow, Edward R., 63

NASA (National Aeronautics and Space Administration)
 aging study by, 93
 Cobb as consultant to, 50, 55, 59–65
 created, 7
 First Women's Space Symposium, 60–61
 testing cancelled by, 56–57
 There's Space for Everyone program, 96–97
 on women in space, 20, 54–55
 See also congressional hearings, Randolph Lovelace,
  Mercury 7, space shuttles, Robert Voas, *and* James Webb

National Organization for Women (NOW), 93–96
Nichols, Nichelle, 96
Nichols, Ruth, 13, 15
Ninety-Nines, 2, 89, 90

O'Brien, Miles, 105
Odlum, Floyd, 70–71

Parade magazine, 52–53, 54, 72
Pirie, Robert B., 55, 70, 73, 77
Powder Puff Derby, 89, 90

race for space, 7, 16, 56, 60
Ratley, Sarah Gorelick. *See* Sarah Gorelick
Reading, Martha Ann, 88
Resnik, Judith, 97–98
Ride, Sally, 94–95, 97–99, 101, 105, 108, 114–115
Right Stuff, Wrong Sex: America's First Women in Space Program
 (Weitekamp), 62
The Right Stuff (Wolfe), v, 8

Sally Ride Science Festival, 108
Seddon, Margaret Rhea, 97–98
Shepard, Alan, 6–7, 31, 61, 73
Shurley, Jay, 24, 25, 26, 27, 29, 51, 84
Skelton, Betty, 11–13, 47
Slayton, Deke, 6–7, 61, 73
Sloan, Jerri, 2, 5, 62, 73, 82, 88, 98, 115, 116–117,
 testing of, 38, 40, 42, 43, 53
social order, changing, 79–80, 85, 87, 95–97
space shuttles, 1–5, 94–95, 96–102, 105
Sputnik, 7
Steadman, Bernice "B," 2, 37, 40, 43, 62, 81, 90, 91, 93, 115,
 116–117

Steinem, Gloria, 96
Still, Susan, 112
Stumbough, Gene Nora, 2, 35, 56, 62, 70, 89–90, 93, 115,
 116–117
 testing of, 39, 40, 41, 53
Sullivan, Kathryn, 97–98, 114

television, women on, 27–29, 95–96, 101
Tereshkova, Valentina, 84, 85
There's Space for Everyone program, 96–97
Thunderbird pilots, 109–111
Time magazine, 72, 90
Tognini, Michel, 4
Truhill, Jerri Sloan. *See* Jerri Sloan

Voas, Robert, 85
Voss, Janice, 112

Walters, Cathryn, 25, 27, 29, 51, 77, 84
water survival test, 47–49
Webb, James, 49–50, 57, 60, 62, 63, 64, 70, 73, 82, 83
Weitekamp, Margaret, ix, 56, 60, 62, 65, 96–97
Whirly-Girls, 2
Whitson, Peggy, 104–105, 113
Williams, Sunita, 115
Wolfe, Tom, v, 8
Woltman, Rhea Hurrle. *See* Rhea Hurrle
Woman in Space Earliest (WISE), 13–15
Woman in Space program, 11, 15–16, 36
 Cochran against, 70–75
 congressional hearings on, 66–70, 73–82
 testing for, 16–20, 35–43
women
 equality for, 69, 96, 105, 108–109
 fighter pilots, 109–111
 stereotypes of, 11–13, 20, 54
 on television, 27–29, 95–96, 101
 testing, astronaut, 11–43
Women Airforce Service Pilots (WASP), 2, 9, 10, 21, 39, 69,
 74, 75, 88
Women's Advisory Committee on Aviation, 93
Women's Army Corps (WAC), 9
women's liberation movement, 96
World War II, 2, 9–10, 21, 75, 88

Yeager, Chuck, 71

Zumwalt, Elmo, 101

Acknowledgments

A book like this cannot be completed without extensive research, which inevitably draws in others who share an author's passion for a subject. I owe great thanks to the many curators, librarians, and researchers who helped me gather the documents and images that brought this story to life. Special thanks go to Margaret Weitekamp from the Smithsonian National Air and Space Museum, Cathryn Walters Liberson, Toni Mullee at the International Women's Air and Space Museum, Tracey MacGowan and Dawn Letson at the Texas Woman's University Libraries, Peggy Powell at the University of Vermont Library Research Annex, and Margie Richison and Carolyn Smith at the Ninety-Nines Museum of Women Pilots, as well as research assistants Stacy Fullerton and Anita Russell. Thank you also to female aviators Betty Skelton and Nicole Malachowski for taking time to talk with me and for staying in touch when questions lingered.

I am thankful, too, for my many writer friends who encouraged me to pursue this story over the years, especially Sarah Aronson, whose belief in the work triggered her matchmaking gene and caused her to tell Marc Aronson (no relation) about my manuscript. And in turn to Marc, who became my editor and guided me with insightful questions that I needed to answer for myself in order to fully realize this story. Thanks also to the wonderful team at Candlewick — especially editor Hilary Van Dusen and designer Sherry Fatla — for taking great care in turning this labor of love into a reality. And to my agent, Rosemary Stimola, for her wisdom and finesse.

And, as always, thank you to my best friend and husband, Alan, and to our children. I am in awe of my family's unconditional love and support, as well as their real understanding that sometimes dinner just has to wait.

Last, I will forever be grateful to the women dubbed the "Mercury 13," as well as their families, for being so welcoming and generous with their time, their stories, and mostly, their hearts. Long may they fly.